Introduction

Judy Yeager is the author of The Southern Lady Cooks website at thesouthernladycooks.com and the Facebook page at www.facebook.com/thesouthernladycooks. Judy is a mom and grandmother that loves to cook, write, garden and work in the yard. Judy is retired from the state of Kentucky where she was employed for twenty seven years. The Southern Lady Cooks website was started in 2008 with traditional Southern recipes, along with family recipes, and dishes created in her Kentucky kitchen.

Judy believes that Southern cooking is a labor of love passed down from one generation to another and you cannot leave a Southern home without eating a meal or having a glass of sweet, iced tea and visiting for a "spell".

This collection of "Down Home Dishes" will be our second cookbook and we are excited to share with you more than 150 amazing recipes. We are so pleased that you loved our first publication,"Sweet Things". We hope you enjoy Down Home Dishes just as much and it will remain in your family for many years.

Best wishes for more great Southern dishes!

Dedication: To all the wonderful people that follow The Southern Lady Cooks website and have become like family to us.

Appreciation: Our appreciation goes to The Southern Lady Cooks followers. We appreciate each and everyone of you and thank you for helping us make this site successful by trying the recipes, sharing with friends and family and traveling along with us on this journey. Cooking makes us happy and remember, "Come rain or come shine, it's going to be a beautiful day"!

Table of Contents

Casseroles	7
Side Dishes	51
Skillet Meals	67
Slow Cooker Recipes	95
Other Main Dishes	135

Casseroles

Cheesy Hash Brown Casserole

8 slices bacon, cooked and drained (keep about 2 tablespoons of the bacon drippings)
1 (30 ounce) bag frozen Country Style shredded hash browns, defrosted
1/2 cup chopped onion, regular or green onions
1 large clove of garlic, chopped
1 teaspoon salt
1/2 teaspoon black pepper
1 (10.75 ounce) can Cream of Potato Soup
1 cup sour cream
3 tablespoons butter or margarine, melted
1 cup evaporated milk (could use regular milk)
25 Ritz crackers, crushed
2 cups shredded cheese of your choice

Fry bacon, drain and set aside. Brown onion and garlic in 2 tablespoons of the bacon grease. Spray a 9 x 13 inch baking dish with cooking spray. In a large bowl blend together by hand the hash browns, onions, garlic, potato soup, salt, pepper, sour cream, milk and melted butter. Spread in casserole dish. Crush Ritz crackers (I put mine in a Ziploc bag and use rolling pin) and break bacon into pieces. Mix cracker crumbs, shredded cheese and bacon together and sprinkle on top of the casserole. Bake in preheated 350 degree oven 45 to 50 minutes. Makes 10 to 12 servings.

Pineapple Casserole

1 (20 ounce) can crushed pineapple, drained (save 1/4 cup juice)
1 (15 ounce) can mandarin oranges, drained
1/2 cup white granulated sugar
6 tablespoons all-purpose flour
1 cup shredded coconut (optional)
2 cups shredded cheddar cheese
1/4 cup pineapple juice from the crushed pineapple above
1 stick butter or margarine or 8 tablespoons or 1/2 cup, melted
40 to 50 Ritz crackers, crushed
1 cup pecans or walnuts (optional)

In a large mixing bowl combine the crushed pineapple, mandarin oranges, sugar, flour, coconut, shredded cheese and pineapple juice. Mix well. Spray a 2 quart baking dish with cooking spray and spread pineapple mixture into the dish. Melt the butter and mix with the crushed Ritz crackers. Sprinkle on top of the pineapple. Add pecans on top. Bake in preheated 350 degree oven 30 to 35 minutes until brown on top. Makes 6 to 8 servings.

Note: You can substitute another 20 ounce can of pineapple chunks or cherries, peaches or whatever fruit you like in place of the mandarin oranges. This dish is good served hot or cold.

American Shepherds Pie

1 to 1 1/2 pounds hamburger
2 tablespoons all-purpose flour
1/2 cup chopped green onions (could use regular onion)
1/2 cup chopped celery
1/2 teaspoon thyme
1 teaspoon basil leaves
1/2 teaspoon minced garlic
1/2 teaspoon black pepper
1/2 teaspoon salt
2 teaspoons Worcestershire sauce
1 tablespoon ketchup
Pinch cayenne or a few drops hot sauce
1 (15 1/4 ounce) can whole kernel corn, drained or two cups frozen corn
1 cup frozen peas
3 cups leftover mashed potatoes
1 1/2 to 2 cups shredded cheese of your choice

Break hamburger into a large skillet and sprinkle the flour over it. Add the onion and celery and brown. Drain if needed. Sprinkle on thyme, basil, garlic, black pepper and salt. Add Worcestershire sauce, ketchup and hot sauce along with corn and peas. Simmer about 15 or 20 minutes. Pour into a sprayed 9 x 13 casserole dish. Spread mashed potatoes over top. (Leftover potatoes spread better if heated some in the microwave if they have been refrigerated). Sprinkle on shredded cheese. Bake in preheated 400 degree oven for 25 to 30 minutes until cheese is melted and casserole is bubbling. Makes 10 to 12 servings.

Baked Chicken with Peaches

1 package chicken parts of your choice
3 tablespoons all-purpose flour
1/2 teaspoon salt
1/4 teaspoon pepper
1/2 teaspoon ground cinnamon
1/2 teaspoon ground nutmeg
2 tablespoons butter or margarine
1 (1 pound) can sliced or halved peaches in juice

In a bowl mix together the flour, salt, pepper, cinnamon and nutmeg. Spray a casserole dish with cooking spray. Place chicken parts in the casserole dish and sprinkle flour mixture over the parts. Cut the butter into pats and put it on top of each chicken piece. Bake uncovered in a preheated 375 degree oven for 35 to 40 minutes. Remove from oven and place peaches in casserole with chicken. Pour the peach juice over the chicken and peaches and put back in oven for 20 more minutes. Remove and spoon juice over chicken and serve.

Note: I use chicken thighs, but you can use whatever part of the chicken you desire.

Baked Sweet Potato Casserole

4 medium to large sweet potatoes, cooked and peeled. I boil mine. You could also use canned sweet potatoes, drained, two of the tall 40 ounce cans
1 stick butter or 1/2 cup or 8 tablespoons
1/4 cup heavy cream (could use evaporated milk or regular milk)
1/2 cup brown sugar
1 egg
1 teaspoon vanilla extract
1/4 teaspoon ground cinnamon (can use more of the spices if you like. I like to taste the sweet potatoes)
1/8 teaspoon nutmeg
1 cup nuts, chopped (walnuts or pecans)
Marshmallows (optional)

Cook and peel sweet potatoes and mash with potato masher. Add butter and cream to potatoes just like if mashing regular potatoes. Stir in brown sugar, egg, vanilla, cinnamon and nutmeg. Spray a casserole dish with cooking spray. I use a 7 x 11 casserole dish. Put mashed sweet potatoes in dish and sprinkle nuts over the top. Bake in preheated 350 degree oven for 35 to 40 minutes. Remove from oven and add enough marshmallows to cover top of baking dish. Can use the miniature or big marshmallows. Put back in oven until marshmallows start to melt and brown on top. I just stick mine under the broiler for a few minutes. This makes 8 to 10 servings. Reheats well in the microwave or oven and could be put together the night before without the nuts and marshmallows and cooked the next day.

Baked Sweet Potatoes

Casserole Ingredients:
2 – 3 large sweet potatoes, boiled, peeled and mashed
1/4 cup butter or margarine
1/4 cup milk
1 egg, beaten
1 teaspoon vanilla extract
1/4 teaspoon nutmeg
1/2 teaspoon cinnamon
2 tablespoons sorghum molasses or molasses of your choice (optional)
1/2 cup sugar

Topping Ingredients:
1/2 cup brown sugar
1/2 cup all-purpose flour
1/2 cup butter or margarine, cut into pieces
1/2 cup walnut or pecan pieces

Cover sweet potatoes with water in a pot and boil until done. Immediately run cold water over the potatoes to stop the cooking process. Peel and mash with hand potato masher. Add butter, sugar, milk, vanilla, nutmeg, cinnamon, molasses and beaten egg. Stir well. Pour into a sprayed 9 x 9 inch casserole dish.

Mix together the topping ingredients in a bowl and sprinkle over the sweet potatoes.

Bake in preheated 375 degree oven 35 to 45 minutes. Makes 6 servings.

Barley Casserole

1/2 cup butter or margarine or 1 stick or 8 tablespoons
1 cup quick cooking barley
1 medium onion chopped
1/2 cup slivered almonds
1 (2 oz. pkg) dehydrated onion soup
2 cups chicken broth
1 (3 oz. can) drained mushroom slices (reserve liquid)
1 (5 oz. can) water chestnuts, drained and sliced

Heat butter in saucepan, add barley and onion and saute till golden color. Add almonds, dry onion soup and chicken broth. Saute mushrooms a few minutes in a little butter and add to barley along with water chestnuts and liquid drained from canned mushrooms. Stir well, pour into a greased casserole dish. Cover and bake at 350 degrees for 1 hour adding more liquid if needed. Makes 8 servings.

Broccoli Casserole

1 (32 ounce) package frozen broccoli cuts, cooked according to package directions
1/2 cup of butter or margarine or 8 tablespoons, melted
1 1/2 sleeves of Ritz crackers (can use more), crumbled
1/2 to 3/4 of a 32 ounce package of Velveeta cheese, cut in chunks
1/2 teaspoon salt
1/4 teaspoon black pepper

Cook broccoli cuts according to package directions. (I cook mine in a bowl in the microwave covered with saran wrap. Add 1/2 the melted butter, salt and pepper, and the Velveeta cheese chunks to the broccoli. Stir to melt. Add the other half of the melted butter to the Ritz cracker crumbs. Spray a 2 quart casserole dish and add a layer of the broccoli and cheese on the bottom. Next add a layer of the buttered crumbs. Continue to do this ending with the top covered with the buttered crumbs. Bake in a preheated 375 degree oven for 15 to 20 minutes until the top is browned. Makes 8 to 10 servings.

Cabbage Roll Casserole

1 pound ground beef
1 medium onion, chopped
2 teaspoons minced garlic
1/2 medium sized head of cabbage, coarsely chopped
1 cup rice, uncooked
1 (8 ounce) can tomato sauce
1 (14.5 ounce) can diced tomatoes, undrained
1 (14.5 ounce) can beef broth
1/4 teaspoon ground thyme
1/2 teaspoon black pepper
1 teaspoon salt
2 tablespoons vinegar, white or apple cider
2 teaspoons Worcestershire sauce
3 tablespoons white granulated sugar
2 cups shredded cheese of your choice

Brown hamburger, onion and minced garlic in a skillet on top of the stove, drain. Whisk together in a bowl until well mixed tomato sauce, diced tomatoes, beef broth, thyme, black pepper, salt, vinegar, Worcestershire sauce and sugar. Spray a 9 x 13 baking dish with cooking spray and add half the chopped cabbage, half the ground beef and onions, half the rice and half the liquid tomato mixture for the first layer. Make a second layer and pour on the remaining liquid mixture. Bake in preheated 350 degree oven, uncovered, for 1 1/2 hours or 90 minutes. Remove from oven and sprinkle cheese over top. Put back into oven for about 20 minutes to melt the cheese. Makes about 8 to 10 servings.

Note: Make sure you mash the rice down on the top layer so that it is wet and not dry. You can cover the last hour if you think the rice is not cooking or getting soft. I make this most of the time with long grain rice and it is always done in my oven at about 90 minutes.

Cabbage, Ham and Spaghetti Casserole

8 ounces of thin spaghetti, cooked al dente according to package directions and drained
6 to 7 cups of chopped cabbage, uncooked
2 cups of cooked, chopped ham
1 medium onion, coarsely chopped or 1 1/2 to 2 cups
1/2 cup butter or margarine or 8 tablespoons or 1 stick
1/3 cup all-purpose flour
1/2 teaspoon black pepper
1/2 teaspoon salt, optional
1 cup milk (I used 2%)
1 (10 3/4 ounce) can cream of mushroom soup, undiluted
2 cups shredded cheese of your choice
1 cup bread crumbs (optional)

Combine butter, flour, pepper, salt, milk and cream of mushroom soup in a saucepan on top of the stove. Bring to a slow boil. Remove and stir in shredded cheese until melted. Spray a 9 x 13 casserole dish. Mix the chopped onion and cabbage together. Layer half the cabbage and onion in the bottom of the dish; add half the cooked spaghetti. Sprinkle on 1 cup of the cooked ham. Pour on half the cheese soup mixture. Make another layer ending with the soup. Cover with foil and bake in preheated 350 degree oven for 60 minutes. Remove foil and sprinkle on bread crumbs and more cheese if desired. Return to oven until cheese melts. (I just put it under the broiler for a few minutes). Makes 10 to 12 servings.

Note: You could make this using about any kind of meat in the casserole.

Cheesy Bacon Yellow Squash Casserole

4 or 5 small to medium yellow squash, unpeeled and sliced in round pieces
4 slices bacon, cooked crisp, drained and crumbled (save drippings)
1/3 cup olive oil
1/4 teaspoon black pepper
1/2 teaspoon salt
1/2 teaspoon dried basil or 1 1/2 teaspoons fresh chopped basil
1/2 teaspoon dried parsley or 1 1/2 teaspoons fresh chopped parsley
1/2 teaspoon minced garlic
2 teaspoons white granulated sugar
1 tablespoon bacon drippings
1/4 cup chopped onion (I use purple onion but can use regular or green onions)
1 cup White Cheddar Cheese-It Cracker crumbs (could use Ritz or Cheddar Cheese-It Crackers)
1 cup shredded cheddar cheese

Slice squash and set aside. Cook bacon, drain and set aside saving drippings. In a bowl combine and whisk together the olive oil, black pepper, salt, basil, parsley, garlic, sugar, bacon drippings and chopped onion. Pour over squash and toss to cover all the squash. Spread a layer of the squash in a 2 to 3 quart baking dish, sprinkle on half the cheese cracker crumbs, half the crumbled bacon and half the shredded cheese. Top with another layer of squash, cracker crumbs, bacon and cheese. Bake covered with foil in a preheated 350 oven for 50 to 55 minutes until squash is done. Makes 6 to 8 servings.

Cheesy Tater Tot Casserole

1 pound hamburger
1 cup chopped onion
1/2 teaspoon parsley flakes
1/2 teaspoon garlic powder
1/2 teaspoon celery seed (you could use chopped celery)
Pinch of cayenne or a few drops of hot sauce
1 (10 3/4 ounce) can cream of mushroom soup, undiluted
1 cup sour cream
1 (15 1/4 ounce) can whole kernel corn, drained (can use fresh or frozen)
2 cups shredded cheese of your choice
About 1/2 of a 32 ounce bag of frozen tater tots

In a skillet on top of the stove add the hamburger, onion, parsley flakes, garlic powder, celery seed and hot sauce. Brown until hamburger is done. Drain. Spread cooked hamburger in the bottom of a 2 quart casserole dish. Mix the cream of mushroom soup and the sour cream together and spread over the hamburger and onions. Next, spread the drained corn over the soup and sprinkle the 2 cups of shredded cheese over the corn. Lay the tater tots on the top. Bake in a preheated 425 degree oven for 25 to 30 minutes until "tots" are nice and brown. Makes 8 to 10 servings.

Note: You could do this with sausage or chicken, too

Cheesy Tuna Casserole

3 cups uncooked medium pasta shells, cooked according to package directions for about 9 minutes and drained
2 (5 ounce) cans tuna, drained
1/4 cup chopped onion (can use regular or green onions)
1 cup frozen green peas (could use canned peas)
1 (10 3/4 ounce) can cream of mushroom soup
1/2 teaspoon garlic powder
1/4 cup sour cream
1/2 cup milk
2 tablespoons butter or margarine, melted
1/2 teaspoon black pepper
1 (4 ounce) can mushroom pieces, drained
1 cup shredded cheese of choice
Cheese crackers (about one cup crumbled)

Cook pasta according to package directions for about 9 minutes, drain and set aside. Combine all remaining ingredients and mix with a spoon except cheese crackers. Mix in the pasta. Pour into a sprayed casserole dish and crumble cheese crackers on top. Bake in a preheated 400 degree oven 35 to 40 minutes. Makes about 8 servings.

Chicken Tortilla Chip Casserole

4 to 5 cups chicken, cooked and chopped
1 cup chopped green onion (can use regular onion)
1 cup chopped green pepper
2 tablespoons oil
1 (14.5 ounce) can diced tomatoes, undrained
1 (10.5 ounce) can cream of celery soup
1 (10.5 ounce) can cream of chicken soup
1 (4 ounce) can green chilies, drained
1/2 teaspoon chili powder
1/2 teaspoon garlic powder
1/2 teaspoon black pepper
1/2 teaspoon salt
1/2 teaspoon cumin
3 to 4 cups crushed tortilla chips
2 cups shredded cheese of your choice

You will need a large skillet. Cook the green pepper and onion in the oil. Add the tomatoes, celery soup, chicken soup, green chilies, chili powder, garlic powder, pepper, salt and cumin to the skillet. Mix well with a spoon and simmer about 10 minutes. Add a layer of crushed tortilla chips to a 9 x 13 baking dish. Next, add a layer of chicken and cover with half the soup mixture from your skillet. Sprinkle on 1 cup of the shredded cheese. Add another layer of chips, chicken, and the rest of the soup mixtures. Bake in a preheated 350 degree oven for 20 to 25 minutes. Remove and add remaining cup of cheese. Return to oven for about 5 minutes or long enough to melt the cheese on top of the casserole dish. Makes 10 to 12 servings.

Note: You can add some cayenne or hot sauce to this casserole if you like hot food. Can serve with a dollop of sour cream on top, chopped tomatoes, olives, etc.

Creamy Cauliflower Casserole

1 small head cauliflower, washed and broken into pieces
1 (10 3/4 ounce) can cream of celery soup, undiluted
1/4 to 1/2 cup green onion, chopped
1/2 cup milk
2 tablespoons all-purpose flour
2 tablespoons sesame seed, toasted
4 tablespoons slivered almonds, toasted
1/2 teaspoon black pepper
1 cup sharp cheddar cheese, divided
Salt to taste

Wash cauliflower and break into pieces. Place in a sprayed casserole with about 1/4 cup water, covered with saran wrap and cook in microwave for about 6 minutes. While cauliflower is cooking, place almonds and sesame seed on a baking sheet and bake in preheated 350 degree oven for 10 minutes. Remove cauliflower from microwave, drain and return to casserole. Combine remaining ingredients except for 1/2 cup cheese, almonds and sesame seeds and pour over cauliflower. Mix with spoon. Sprinkle remaining 1/2 cup cheese on top and sprinkle almonds and sesame seed over casserole. Bake in preheated 400 degree oven for 30 minutes. Makes 6 to 8 servings.

Easy Cheesy Breakfast Casserole

1/2 pound pork sausage, cooked and drained
1/4 cup all-purpose flour
1/4 teaspoon salt
1/4 teaspoon black pepper
1/4 cup or 4 tablespoons butter or margarine, melted
4 eggs
1 cup cottage cheese
1 1/2 cups shredded cheddar cheese
1 (4 ounce) can green chilies, drained
1 (4 ounce) jar pimento, drained
1/4 cup chopped green pepper

Cook sausage, drain and set aside. Whisk together flour, salt, pepper, butter, eggs and cottage cheese in a large bowl. Generously spray an 8 x 8 baking dish. Pour in egg mixture and sprinkle cooked sausage over top. Sprinkle on the cheese and add pimento, chilies and green pepper. Bake in preheated 375 degree oven for 35 minutes.   Makes 6 to 8 servings.

Garlic Cheese Grits

1 1/2 cups uncooked instant, quick cooking or regular grits
1 stick butter or margarine or 1/2 cup, or 8 tablespoons
12 oz. Velveeta cheese or cheddar cheese
1 tablespoon garlic powder
3 eggs
1 cup milk
small cheese crackers

Cook 1 1/2 cups instant or regular grits according to package directions. Remove from stove, add one stick butter or margarine and the garlic powder. Cut cheese into chunks and add to grits. Beat 3 eggs and 1 cup milk together and add to grits and cheese. Spray casserole dish and add mixture. Top with crushed cheese crackers. Bake at 350 degrees for 40 minutes or until knife comes out clean when inserted.

Note: You can use any cheese you like. If you are not a garlic fan, you can use a smaller amount.

Ham, Potato and Broccoli Casserole

6 or 7 medium potatoes, peeled and thinly sliced or cut in bite-sized chunks
2 cups chopped ham, cooked
2 cups chopped broccoli, fresh or frozen
1/3 cup chopped green onions, could use regular onions
1 (10 3/4 ounce) can cream of broccoli soup, undiluted
1/2 cup sour cream
1/4 cup mayonnaise
1 teaspoon dried chives
1 tablespoon grated Parmesan cheese
1 teaspoon black pepper
1 teaspoon salt (optional)
1/2 teaspoon garlic powder
4 tablespoons butter or margarine, melted or 1/4 cup
1 cup shredded cheddar cheese or cheese or your choice

Combine potatoes, ham, broccoli, onions in a sprayed 3 quart casserole dish.
In a bowl mix together soup, sour cream, mayonnaise, chives, Parmesan
cheese, pepper, salt, garlic power and melted butter. Stir with a spoon to mix
well. Pour over potatoes, ham, broccoli and onions and mix. Cover with foil
and bake in preheated 400 degree oven for 45 minutes to an hour until
potatoes are cooked when you stick a fork in them. Remove and sprinkle the
cup of shredded cheese over top. Leave off foil and bake another 10 minutes
uncovered. Makes about 10 servings.

Ham, Spinach and Pasta Casserole

2 cups uncooked pasta
2 tablespoons butter
1/2 cup chopped onion
1 teaspoon minced garlic
2 cups chopped fresh baby spinach (could use frozen)
2 tablespoons all-purpose flour
1 1/2 cups milk
1/2 teaspoon black pepper
1 teaspoon salt
1/2 cup sour cream
2 cups cooked chopped ham
1 1/2 cups shredded Parmesan cheese
1 cup Ritz cracker crumbs

Cook pasta according to package directions, drain and set aside. Brown onion in butter, add garlic and baby spinach and cook about five minutes until spinach is tender. Remove spinach and onions and set aside. Add the flour to the butter like you were making a roux or gravy, stir in milk, black pepper, salt and sour cream. Stir until smooth. Remove from heat and stir in the pasta, ham and Parmesan cheese along with the spinach and onions. Pour into a sprayed casserole dish, sprinkle on Ritz cracker crumbs. Bake in preheated 350 degree oven for 30 to 35 minutes until crackers are browned on top. Makes about 8 servings.

Hamburger 'N Shells Italia

2 cups medium sized pasta shells, uncooked
1 pound hamburger
1 small onion, chopped or 1 cup
1/2 teaspoon black pepper
1 teaspoon minced garlic
1 tablespoon dried Italian seasoning (could use Oregano, too)
1 teaspoon salt
2 (8 ounce) cans tomato sauce
1 (13.25 ounce) can mushroom stems and pieces, drained
2 cups small curd cottage cheese
2 cups shredded cheddar cheese

Cook the pasta shells according to package directions to the al dente stage, drain and set aside. In a skillet brown the hamburger and onion, add pepper, garlic, Italian seasoning, salt and mushrooms. Drain hamburger. Add the shells to the hamburger mixture along with the tomato sauce. Spray a 2 quart casserole dish. Spread a layer of the hamburger in the bottom of the dish. Spread a cup of the cottage cheese over the hamburger followed by a cup of the shredded cheese. Add a second layer ending with cheese on top. Bake in a preheated 350 degree oven about 35 to 40 minutes until bubbly. Makes about 8 to 10 servings.

Hamburger Supreme Casserole

1 pound ground beef
1/2 cup chopped onion
1 (10.5 ounce) can cream of mushroom soup
1/2 cup milk
1/2 teaspoon minced garlic
1/2 teaspoon salt
1/4 teaspoon black pepper
1/4 teaspoon thyme
1 (4 ounce) can mushrooms, drained
2 cups macaroni, uncooked
8 ounces sharp cheddar cheese grated or shredded

Brown meat and onion with garlic until tender in skillet on top of stove. Cook macaroni according to package directions, drain and set aside. Drain hamburger mixture and stir in soup, milk, seasonings, and mushrooms. Layer half of hamburger, macaroni and cheese in a 2 quart casserole. Repeat with meat and macaroni. Save last half of cheese. Bake in preheated 350 degree oven for 20 minutes. Sprinkle with remaining cheese. Return to oven until cheese melts. Makes 6 to 8 servings.

Hash Brown and Sausage Breakfast Casserole

2 lbs. frozen hash browns
1 medium onion, chopped
1 green pepper, chopped
2 lbs. pork sausage, cooked
10 eggs beaten
Salt and pepper to taste
1/2 teaspoon garlic powder (optional)
1 1/2 cups shredded cheddar cheese
Oil for cooking hash browns

Heat oil, add hash browns, onion and peppers. Cook till potatoes begin to brown. Spray 9 x 13 baking dish with cooking spray. Spread potato mixture in pan, top with cooked sausage or ham. Pour beaten eggs over all and season with salt and pepper and garlic. Gently stir to coat all ingredients with eggs. Sprinkle with cheese. Bake uncovered at 375 degrees for 35 to 40 minutes. Makes 8 servings.

Note: You can refrigerate overnight and then bake. You can use any kind of meat you like.

Hawaiian Beans and Wieners

1/2 stick butter or 4 tablespoons or 1/4 cup
1/2 cup chopped onion
1/3 cup chopped green pepper
1 (20 ounce) can pineapple rings, reserve syrup
1 package wieners or franks or brats, cut in bite-sized pieces
2 tablespoons vinegar (I use white distilled vinegar)
2 tablespoons soy sauce
2/3 cup brown sugar
1/3 cup tomato ketchup
2 (1 pound) cans pork and beans, drained

Cut the pineapple into chunks reserving the juice and 4 rings for garnish. In a skillet cook green pepper, onion, pineapple chunks, and wieners in the butter until onion and green pepper is cooked and the pineapple and wieners are beginning to get browned. Add the reserved pineapple syrup to skillet along with vinegar, soy sauce, brown sugar and ketchup. Heat until begins to bubble. Pour drained pork and beans into a two quart casserole dish, add ingredients in skillet and mix together. Place the remaining pineapple rings on top and bake in preheated 350 degree oven for 30 to 40 minutes. Makes 6 to 8 servings.

Hearty Chicken Pot Pie

Casserole Ingredients:
2 boneless, skinless chicken breasts
1 cup chopped celery
1 small onion, chopped
3 or 4 medium sized carrots,
chopped
3 or 4 medium potatoes, peeled and
chopped
1/4 teaspoon black pepper
1/2 teaspoon minced garlic
1/2 teaspoon salt
4 tablespoons butter or 1/4 cup
1 (15 ounce) can mixed vegetables or
veg-all, drained
1 (10 3/4 ounce) can cream of
chicken soup, undiluted
3/4 cup chicken broth
1/2 teaspoon ground thyme

Topping Ingredients:
1 cup original Bisquick
1/2 cup evaporated milk
1 egg

Cut chicken breasts into bite-sized pieces. Melt butter in skillet on top of stove and add onions, celery, chicken pieces, pepper, garlic, and salt. Saute until onions and celery is tender and chicken is cooked. While chicken is cooking place carrots and potatoes in 2 quart casserole dish and cook in microwave for 8 to 10 minutes on high until tender. Remove casserole from microwave and add cooked chicken, onions, and celery to carrots and potatoes.Pour in mixed vegetables. In a bowl combine the chicken soup and chicken broth and thyme and whisk together. Pour over casserole and mix with a spoon. In a separate bowl mix the Bisquick, evaporated milk, and egg. Whisk well. Pour over vegetables and spread evenly over the top. Bake in a preheated 400 degree oven for 30 – 40 minutes until golden brown on top. Makes 6 to 8 servings.

Note: You can make this with ham, hamburger, and beef, too.

Hearty Mexican Casserole

Casserole Ingredients:
1 1/2 pounds ground beef
12 ounce package frozen corn
1 medium onion, chopped
1 green pepper, chopped
1 (15 ounce can) tomato sauce
1/4 cup water
1 (4 ounce can) chopped green chilies, drained
1 (15 ounce can) black beans, drained
1/4 teaspoon black pepper
1/2 teaspoon salt
1/2 teaspoon cumin
1/4 teaspoon dried cilantro
1/4 teaspoon chili powder
Shredded cheese of your choice

Cornbread Topping:
1 cup self-rising cornmeal
1/4 cup all-purpose flour
2/3 cup milk
1 egg

Brown ground beef, onion, and green pepper in skillet on top of the stove. Drain. Combine the rest of the ingredients and pour into a 9 x 13 baking dish. Mix cornbread topping and drop by spoonfuls on top of casserole. Bake in preheated 425 degree oven 20 to 25 minutes until cornbread topping is done. Remove from oven and add shredded cheese and melt under broiler.

To make Cornbread Topping stir all cornbread ingredients in a bowl with a spoon.

Makes 6 to 8 servings.

Italian Eggplant Casserole

1 medium eggplant peeled and diced in 1 inch pieces or 3 to 4 cups
1 pound lean hamburger
1 cup coarsely chopped onion
1 cup coarsely chopped green pepper
1/2 teaspoon black pepper
1/2 teaspoon salt
1 teaspoon dried oregano
1 teaspoon minced garlic
2 teaspoons Worcestershire sauce
Pinch of cayenne or several drops of hot sauce
1 tablespoon fresh basil, chopped (optional)
1 (14.5 ounce) can diced tomatoes or could use about 2 cups fresh tomatoes, diced
4 tablespoons Italian bread crumbs or plain bread crumbs
1 cup Italian Style shredded cheese

Cook the eggplant in enough water to cover it for about 10 minutes until tender. Remove, drain and set aside. In a skillet cook the hamburger, chopped onion, chopped green pepper along with black pepper, salt, oregano, garlic, Worcestershire sauce, cayenne and basil until hamburger is browned and onions and peppers are cooked. Drain the hamburger. Stir in tomatoes and eggplant. Spray a baking dish (2 to 3 quart size) with cooking spray, add half of the eggplant and hamburger mixture, sprinkle on 2 tablespoons of the bread crumbs, add 1/2 cup cheese. Spread on the other half of the hamburger and eggplant mixture, add the last two tablespoons of bread crumbs and the last 1/2 cup shredded cheese (can add more bread crumbs and cheese if you like) Bake in preheated 350 degree oven 20 to 25 minutes. Makes 6 to 8 servings.

Mashed Potato Casserole

7 or 8 large potatoes, peeled
1 teaspoon salt
4 tablespoons butter or margarine
4 ounces cream cheese
1/4 cup sour cream
1/2 cup evaporated milk
1/2 teaspoon black pepper
1 teaspoon onion flakes
1/4 teaspoon garlic powder
1 to 2 cups Monterey Jack cheese, shredded or cheese of your choice
1 teaspoon paprika

Boil the peeled potatoes, drain and mash with the salt, butter, cream cheese, sour cream, milk, pepper, onion flakes and garlic. Spread mashed potatoes into a sprayed casserole dish and sprinkle with shredded cheese and paprika. Bake in preheated 375 degree oven, uncovered, for 30 to 35 minutes. Makes 6 to 8 servings.

Note: You can add chopped bacon or ham, regular onion or green onion

Ritzy Brussels Sprouts

1 (16 ounce) bag frozen brussels sprouts, cooked according to package directions.
1 (10.5 ounce) can cream of celery soup
1/4 cup milk (I use 2%)
1 teaspoon minced onion
1/2 teaspoon garlic powder
1/2 teaspoon black pepper
1/2 cup Ritz cracker crumbs (could use more)
1/2 cup shredded cheddar cheese or cheese of your choice
3 or 4 tablespoons slivered almonds

Cook brussels sprouts according to package directions, drain. Spray 1 quart casserole dish and add brussels sprouts. In a bowl combine soup, milk, minced onion, garlic powder and pepper. Pour over the brussels sprouts. Sprinkle Ritz crumbs, cheese and almonds on top. Bake uncovered in preheated 400 degree oven for 30 to 35 minutes. Makes about 6 servings.

Salmon Pasta Casserole

1 (14 3/4 ounce can) pink salmon, drained and flaked
1/3 to 1/2 of a pound box of spaghetti, cooked according to package directions
2 tablespoons butter or margarine
1/2 cup chopped green pepper
1/2 cup chopped green onions (can use regular onions)
1/2 cup chopped celery
1 (10 3/4 ounce) can cream of mushroom soup, undiluted
1/2 cup sour cream
1 (4 ounce) can sliced mushrooms, drained
1/2 teaspoon black pepper
1/4 teaspoon sage
1/8 teaspoon thyme
Pinch cayenne
Ritz crackers, crushed (about 10)
1 cup shredded cheddar cheese

Cook spaghetti according to package directions to al dente stage, drain, set aside. Melt butter in skillet on top of stove and cook green pepper, onion and celery until tender. Add salmon, mushroom soup, sour cream, mushrooms, black pepper, sage, thyme and cayenne mixing all together. Cook on medium heat until all ingredients are hot. Spray a casserole dish and layer the spaghetti on bottom, then skillet mixture alternating with spaghetti. Crumble crackers on top and sprinkle with cheese. Bake in preheated 375 degree oven for 30 to 35 minutes. Makes 8 to 10 servings.

Sausage, Tomato and Cheese Grits Casserole

1/2 pound pork sausage
3 cups cooked grits, (can be regular or the quick-cooking grits)
1/2 cup chopped onion
1/2 cup chopped green pepper
1/2 teaspoon salt
1/4 teaspoon black pepper
1 teaspoon minced garlic
2 tablespoons butter, melted
1 (10 ounce) can diced tomatoes with green chilies, undrained
1 1/2 cups shredded cheddar cheese or cheese of your choice

Brown sausage, green pepper and onion in a skillet on top of the stove. Drain. Spray a 2 quart casserole dish with cooking spray. Combine sausage, onion and pepper with cooked grits. Add salt, pepper, garlic, melted butter and diced tomatoes. Stir to mix. Sprinkle cheese on top and bake in preheated 350 degree oven 30 to 35 minutes, uncovered. Makes about 8 servings.

Note: You could use Smoked sausage, or even Italian or Polish in this recipe.

Scalloped Corn Casserole

4 slices bacon, cooked crisp (save drippings)
3 tablespoons bacon drippings
3/4 cup chopped onion (can use regular or green onions)
1/2 cup chopped green pepper
1 sleeve Ritz cracker crumbs or about 2 cups
2 (14.75 ounce) cans cream style sweet corn or 1 can of creamed corn and 1
1/2 cups fresh or frozen whole kernel corn
3 eggs
1 (4 ounce) can pimentos, drained
3/4 cup milk
1/4 teaspoon salt
1/4 teaspoon black pepper
1 cup shredded cheddar cheese

Fry bacon, drain and set aside. Cook onion and green pepper in 3
tablespoons of the bacon drippings then add cracker crumbs to the skillet
with the green pepper and onions and brown just a little. Set this aside.
Combine corn, eggs, pimentos, milk, salt and pepper (mixing with a spoon)
and pour into sprayed 2 quart casserole dish. Sprinkle green peppers, onion
and cracker crumbs over the top. Next, sprinkle on the cheese and crumble
the bacon slices on the cheese. Bake in preheated 350 degree oven for 45 to
50 minutes. Makes 8 to 10 servings.

Scalloped Potatoes with Cheese

1/2 stick butter or 1/4 cup or 4 tablespoons
3 tablespoons all purpose flour
2 1/2 cups milk
1 small onion, chopped
4 or 5 cups sliced and peeled raw potatoes
salt and pepper
Shredded cheese of your choice

Melt butter in skillet; add flour stirring constantly until well mixed. Pour in milk and bring to a rolling boil until milk thickens like a sauce or gravy. Place a layer of potatoes in baking dish. Sprinkle with chopped onion, salt and pepper.

Pour sauce over potatoes. Continue until all potatoes are in dish. Cover and cook in a preheated 350 degree oven for one hour. Remove cover and cook for 30 more minutes. Sprinkle with shredded cheese of your choice. Return to oven until cheese is melted.

Makes 6 to 8 servings.

Swiss Chicken Casserole

4 to 6 chicken breasts, boneless and skinned
4 to 6 slices Swiss cheese
1 (10 1/2 ounce) can Campbell's cream of chicken soup
1/3 cup chopped onion
1 (4 ounce) can mushroom pieces, drained
1 cup milk
1/4 teaspoon black pepper
1/2 teaspoon rubbed sage
1/4 teaspoon ground mustard
1 (14 ounce) can Campbell's chicken gravy
1 (6 ounce) box chicken flavored stuffing mix (I use Kroger brand)
1/2 stick butter or 1/4 cup or 4 tablespoons, melted

Spray a 9 x 13 baking dish or a deep dish casserole with cooking spray. Place chicken breasts in pan and place a slice of swiss cheese on each breast. Mix remaining ingredients in a bowl with a whisk, pour in uncooked stuffing mix and stir. Pour over the chicken. Cook covered in a preheated 350 degree oven for 60 minutes. Remove cover for last 15 to 20 minutes. (If your chicken is frozen when you are putting the casserole together, you should cook about 90 minutes to make sure chicken breasts are done).

Yummy Corn Casserole

2 1/2 cups frozen corn
1 (14.75 ounce) can creamed corn
1 (8 ounce) package cream cheese, softened
1 (4 ounce) can green chilis, drained
1/2 stick of butter or 4 tablespoons, or 1/4 cup, divided
1/2 cup chopped green onion
1/2 cup chopped green or red peppers
1/2 teaspoon salt
1/2 teaspoon paprika
Pinch cayenne or black pepper (optional)
1 (6 ounce) can crispy fried onions

Brown onion and green or red peppers in skillet in one tablespoon of the butter. Spray a 2 quart or larger baking dish with cooking spray. Combine the frozen corn, creamed corn, cream cheese, green chilies, the other 3 tablespoons butter (melted), green onion, green or red peppers, salt, paprika and cayenne or black pepper and add to baking dish. Bake in preheated 350 degree oven for 20 minutes. Remove and stir 1 cup of the crispy fried onions into the casserole. Add the remaining onions on top and bake for 20 more minutes or until onions are golden brown. Makes 8 to 10 servings.

Note: You could add meat to this dish and make it a meal. Cooked meat like smoked sausage, chicken, turkey or ham would all be good in this dish. Bacon would be good, too.

Zucchini and Tomato Casserole

2 medium sized zucchini, unpeeled and thinly sliced
1 medium onion, chopped
2 or 3 medium sized tomatoes, sliced
2 cups cheese, shredded
1 1/2 cups bread crumbs
1 teaspoon oregano
1 teaspoon chili powder
1 teaspoon salt
1/2 teaspoon pepper
1 teaspoon garlic powder
1 teaspoon parsley flakes

In a small bowl mix all the spices and salt and pepper, set aside. Spray a
baking dish with cooking spray (I used a 9 x 9) add a layer of chopped onion,
zucchini slices, tomato slices, cheese, and bread crumbs. Sprinkle with spice
mixture. Continue layering until you run out of ingredients ending with
cheese and bread crumbs on top. Bake in a preheated 375 degree oven,
uncovered, for 45 to 50 minutes. Makes 6 servings.

Note: You could add yellow squash to this recipe, too. Use the shredded
cheese of your choice.

Zucchini Pasta Casserole

4 cups chopped zucchini squash, unpeeled
2 cups shell pasta
1/2 cup chopped purple onion
3 tablespoons butter
3 tablespoons flour
1/2 teaspoon salt
1/4 teaspoon black pepper
1 teaspoon Italian seasoning or could use oregano
1/2 teaspoon minced garlic
1 teaspoon fresh chopped basil or 1/2 teaspoon dried basil (optional)
1/2 teaspoon fresh chopped chives (optional)
2 cups milk
2 cups fresh chopped tomatoes or canned tomatoes
1 cup chopped ham, cooked
1/3 cup bread crumbs
1 cup shredded Parmesan cheese, divided 2/3 cup + 1/3 cup

Cook pasta according to package directions to al dente and drain. Set aside. Melt butter in a large skillet. Add squash and onion and saute' until squash starts to get tender. Add flour, salt, pepper, Italian seasoning, minced garlic, basil, chives and milk. Cook till starts to thicken. Stir in 2/3 cup of the Parmesan cheese and the pasta. Add the tomatoes and ham. Mix to combine all ingredients. Remove from stove and pour into a 2 to 3 quart baking dish. Sprinkle bread crumbs and the other 1/3 cup Parmesan cheese on top. Bake in preheated 350 degree oven, uncovered, 30 to 35 minutes. Makes about 8 servings.

Note: You can use regular or rotini pasta as well as green or regular onion. You can also use chicken or bacon.

Black-Eyed Peas and Smoked Sausage

1 1/2 cups dried black-eyed peas, (cooked according to package directions) or two 14 ounce cans, undrained or you could use frozen peas.
1 small onion, chopped
1/2 cup brown sugar
1 tablespoon spicy brown mustard
2 tablespoons tomato ketchup
1 tablespoon molasses or syrup
1/2 cup chopped green pepper
1/2 teaspoon salt
1/4 teaspoon black pepper
1/2 pound smoked sausage, sliced in rounds

Cook dried peas according to package directions leaving about 1/2 cup of the soup and draining the rest. Add the chopped onion, brown sugar, mustard, ketchup, molasses, salt, pepper and sausage. Stir all ingredients together in a 2 quart baking dish and bake covered in a preheated 350 degree oven for 30 minutes. Remove cover and bake another 15 minutes. Makes 6 to 8 servings.

Cheesy Macaroni and Cheese

1 1/2 cups elbow macaroni, cooked according to package directions
2/3 cup evaporated milk
1 egg, beaten
1/3 cup sour cream
1/2 stick of butter or 1/4 cup or 4 tablespoons, softened
2 cups shredded sharp cheddar cheese
1 cup Velveeta cheese or 8 ounces cut into pieces (if you don't like Velveeta, add 3 cups cheddar instead of 2)
1/4 teaspoon black pepper
1/2 teaspoon salt

Cook macaroni according to package directions and drain. Add butter and cheeses to macaroni and mix well Beat egg, milk, sour cream, pepper and salt together with a wire whisk. Add to macaroni and cheese. Spray a casserole dish with cooking spray and add macaroni. Cook covered with foil in a 350 degree preheated oven for 50 to 60 minutes.   This makes about 6 servings. You can double the recipe if needed.

Chicken Salad Casserole

2 cups chopped chicken, cooked
1 can cream of chicken soup, undiluted
1/4 cup chopped onion
1 cup chopped celery
1 cup rice, cooked
1/2 teaspoon salt
black pepper to taste
1 cup sliced water chestnuts
1/4 cup mayonnaise
crushed multi-grain Tortilla Chips

Combine all ingredients but tortilla chips and place in ungreased casserole. Top with crushed Tortilla Chips. Bake at 450 degrees for 30 minutes. Makes about 6 servings.

Note: Can use Instant Brown Rice.

Orange Beet Casserole

2 (14.5 ounce) cans fresh cut sliced beets, drained
2 tablespoons flour
1/2 cup orange juice
2 tablespoons butter or margarine, melted
2 tablespoons sugar
1/2 teaspoon salt
1/2 teaspoon black pepper

Whisk together flour, juice and butter. Make sure flour is dissolved in liquid. Whisk in remaining ingredients. Pour over beets in a 1 quart casserole dish. Bake in preheated 350 degree oven for 30 minutes stirring well after 15 minutes. Makes 6 to 8 servings.

Note: Could use fresh cooked beets too.

Savory Corn Pudding

2 (14.75 ounce) cans white sweet cream style corn
1 cup evaporated milk
3 tablespoons all-purpose flour
4 tablespoons sugar
1/2 stick of butter or 1/4 cup or 4 tablespoons, melted
3 large eggs, beaten

Pour corn into casserole dish. In a separate bowl combine milk, flour, sugar, butter, and eggs. Mix well with whisk. Add to corn in casserole and mix. Bake in preheated 350 degree oven for 1 hour. Stir twice while baking. Once after 20 minutes and again at 40 minutes. Makes 6 to 8 servings.

Spicy Apricot Chicken

4 boneless, skinless chicken breasts, thawed or frozen
1 teaspoon salt
1/2 teaspoon coarse ground black pepper
1 cup Apricot preserves
1/2 cup honey
1 package dry onion soup mix
1/4 teaspoon ginger
1/4 teaspoon ground cloves
1 teaspoon Dijon mustard

Rub salt and pepper into chicken breasts and place into a casserole dish. Mix together remaining ingredients in a bowl and pour over chicken. Cover with lid or Reynolds wrap and bake in preheated 350 degree oven for 1 hour. Serve over rice.

Note: You can use regular ground black pepper.

Sweet Potato Pone

3 to 4 large sweet potatoes, peeled and grated
1/4 stick of butter or 4 tablespoons, softened
1/2 cup brown sugar
2 eggs
1/4 cup molasses
1/2 cup evaporated milk (can use half n half)
1 teaspoon vanilla extract
1/2 teaspoon ground cinnamon
1/4 teaspoon salt
1/2 teaspoon nutmeg
1/8 teaspoon ground cloves

Cream butter and brown sugar with mixer. Add eggs, molasses, milk, vanilla and spices and continue mixing. Fold in shredded sweet potatoes. Bake in sprayed 8 x 8 casserole dish in preheated 300 degree oven about one hour. Makes about 6 to 8 servings.

Side Dishes

Fried Green Tomatoes and Fried Okra

3 or 4 green tomatoes
1/2 cup all-purpose flour or 1/2 cup cornmeal
2 eggs
salt and pepper
dash of garlic powder
1/2 to 3/4 cup cooking oil

Slice green tomatoes into slices about 1/4 inch thick. In a bowl beat eggs with a whisk. In another bowl add salt and pepper and garlic powder to meal or flour whichever you decide to use for breading. There is really not much difference. The tomatoes in the picture have been done with both. I usually have a bowl of flour and a bowl of cornmeal and I do about half the tomatoes in flour and half in meal. You can do the okra the same way or just use either one. Dip the tomato slices into the egg then the meal or flour. Have your oil hot and deep enough in the skillet to cover about half the tomato slice. Cook on one side, turn and continue cooking until a golden brown. Drain on paper towel.

For okra: Cut okra into 1/4 inch pieces and dip into egg and then flour or meal. Cook just like you did the tomatoes.

Makes 4 servings.

Roasted Brussels Sprouts with Bacon and Walnuts

1 to 1 1/2 pounds fresh Brussels sprouts (could use frozen), washed with outer leaves discarded, ends removed and split in half
4 slices bacon
3 or 4 green onions, chopped
1 small sweet red pepper, chopped
1 teaspoon olive oil
sea salt and black pepper
1 cup chopped walnuts (could use pecans)
1/2 cup craisins or could use raisins
2 tablespoons roasted sunflower seeds (optional)
Grated Parmesan cheese (optional)

Fry bacon until crisp, remove from skillet, drain on paper towels, crumble and set aside. Cook red pepper and onion in bacon drippings, drain and set aside with bacon. Add olive oil to skillet with bacon drippings left in pan and toss brussels spouts in oil and drippings. Spray a cookie sheet with cooking oil and spread brussels sprouts out on sheet along with the cup of walnuts. Sprinkle sea salt and black pepper over brussels sprouts. Roast in preheated 425 degree oven for 15 minutes turning once or twice to keep from burning. Remove from oven. Place brussels sprouts and nuts in serving dish along with craisins, crumbled bacon, cooked peppers and onion, sunflower seeds. Sprinkle on grated Parmesan cheese if desired. Makes 6 to 8 servings.

Note: I don't like my brussels sprouts cooked until almost black. If you like them this way, you will need to remove nuts from the pan and cook sprouts a little longer than 15 minutes.

— 55 —

Cornbread Dressing and Giblet Gravy

Dressing Ingredients:
4 cups cornbread crumbs
3 cups biscuit crumbs
1 medium onion, chopped
1 cup chopped celery
1 stick butter or 1/2 cup or 8 tablespoons
1 teaspoon each salt and pepper
1 (14 oz) can chicken broth or 2 cups turkey broth
1 tablespoon sage
1 (10 3/4 oz.) can Campbells Cream of Chicken Soup, undiluted

Giblet Gravy Ingredients:
Giblets from turkey (heart, gizzard, liver and neck)
4 cups water
1 teaspoon salt
1 teaspoon pepper
Drippings from turkey pan (about a cup)
3/4 cup self-rising flour

Dressing Instructions: In a large bowl mix the cornbread and biscuit crumbs, add onion, celery, salt, pepper, sage, and mix well with a spoon. Melt butter and pour over mixture. Add broth and soup and continue mixing. Spray or grease a casserole dish. Add stuffing and bake at 400 degrees for 35 minutes or until brown around the edges. Makes 10 to 12 servings.

Giblet Gravy: Boil giblets in water until cooked. Remove and chop. I remove the skin from the neck and pull any meat off the bone. Discard neck bone. Put meat and giblets back in water and add salt and pepper, flour and drippings. Continue cooking while stirring continuously with wire whisk until thickens. Serve over stuffing or dressing.

Great Deviled Eggs

6 eggs, boiled and peeled
2 teaspoons sweet pickle relish
2 tablespoons mayonnaise
2 tablespoons yellow mustard
1/8 teaspoon black pepper
1/4 teaspoon salt
1/4 teaspoon sugar
Paprika (to sprinkle on top)

Contrary to what many people say, I think adding the eggs to boiling, salted water, makes them easier to peel. Always have eggs at room temperature before boiling! Bring salted water (add about 1 tablespoon salt to water before boiling) to a boil and add eggs. I use a soup ladle to lower the uncooked eggs gently into the boiling water. Boil eggs on medium heat and boil one minute per egg. A dozen eggs takes twelve minutes boiling time. Remove pot from stove and put under cold running water. Peel immediately holding the egg under the cold water for smooth, peeled eggs.

Once peeled, slice the eggs lengthwise and scoop out the center yolks. In a bowl combine egg yolks with ingredients and mash with a fork. Spoon filling into halves. Sprinkle eggs with paprika.

Makes 12 deviled egg halves.

Green Beans and Potatoes

2 pounds fresh, frozen or canned green beans (if fresh, remove ends and break into pieces and wash the beans)
6 or 7 red potatoes, cut in pieces (I have made this using any kind of potatoes)
1 to 2 cups chicken broth or 1 (14.5 ounce) can
1 ham hock
3 cups water
1/2 teaspoon black pepper
1 teaspoon salt
1/2 cup finely diced onion (optional)
1 teaspoon minced garlic (optional)

Combine all ingredients in a large pot, bring to a boil, then turn to medium low and cook about 1 1/2 hours until potatoes are done and water has cooked down. You can also do this in the crock pot and let cook on low 6 to 7 hours or high 4 hours. Makes 8 to 10 servings.

Notes: You can use cooked ham, bacon, pork jowl or salt pork about a half cup, chopped. You can also add a couple teaspoons bacon drippings if you are just using ham. This will add flavor to the beans. I don't peel my potatoes.

Macaroni and Tomatoes

2 cups macaroni, uncooked
1 (14.5 ounce can) petite diced tomatoes
1 (14.5) ounce can) whole tomatoes in juice
1 tablespoon bacon grease (can add more)
Salt to taste
1/2 teaspoon black pepper

Prepare macaroni in boiling, salted water according to package directions. Drain. Return pasta to cooking pot and add the diced tomatoes and whole tomatoes along with the juice. I just break up the whole tomatoes. Add bacon grease, salt and pepper and simmer for about 10 minutes. Makes 8 to 10 servings.

Maple Baked Beans with Sausage

2 large 28 ounce cans of Bush's Original Baked Beans
1 lb of Jimmy Dean Country Mild Sausage
1/2 cup of chopped white onion
2 tablespoons of brown sugar
1 tablespoon of McCormick Grill Mates Smokehouse Maple
2 tablespoons of ketchup
2 tablespoons of mustard
1/3 cup of maple syrup

Brown sausage in skillet and drain grease. Combine sausage with all other ingredients in a casserole dish with lid and bake on 300 degrees in a preheated oven for around 2 hours or until desired consistency. Makes 8 to 10 servings.

Parmesan Baked Potato Wedges

4 to 6 potatoes, peeled and cut into wedges (I make 8 wedges per potato)
1 cup flour
1/2 teaspoon parsley flakes
1/2 teaspoon oregano
Pinch cayenne pepper
1/4 teaspoon paprika
1/4 teaspoon black pepper
1/2 teaspoon salt
1/2 teaspoon garlic powder
1/4 cup grated Parmesan cheese
1 stick butter, melted or 8 tablespoons or 1/2 cup
Cooking spray

In a bowl whisk together the flour, parsley flakes, oregano, cayenne pepper, paprika, black pepper, salt, garlic powder and Parmesan cheese. Spray a baking sheet with cooking spray. Dip the potato wedges in the butter and roll in the flour mixture or put flour mixture in a paper bag, add potato wedges and shake to cover. Arrange on sprayed baking sheet. Bake in preheated 400 degree oven for 20 minutes on each side turning once. (I spray the potatoes with a little cooking spray when I turn them). Makes 4 to 6 servings.

Baked Parmesan Zucchini Fries

3 medium zucchini, unpeeled
1 cup plain bread crumbs
1/2 cup grated Parmesan cheese
1/4 teaspoon salt
1/4 teaspoon black pepper
3/4 teaspoon garlic powder
2 eggs
1/2 cup buttermilk (could use regular milk)
Cooking spray

Cut zucchini in half crosswise and then cut lengthwise into pieces like fries. Combine bread crumbs, cheese, salt, pepper, and garlic powder in a bowl or shallow dish. Beat eggs and milk together. Dip zucchini pieces in egg and milk then dredge in crumbs. Spray baking sheet with cooking spray. Place zucchini fries on sheet and spray the fries with cooking spray. Bake in preheated 400 degree oven 35 to 40 minutes until brown and crusty. Turn if needed. Makes about 6 servings.

Brown Sugar Glazed Baby Carrots

16 ounces baby carrots
2 tablespoons butter or margarine
1/3 cup brown sugar
1 cup water
dash salt
1/2 teaspoon ground ginger
1/2 teaspoon ground allspice
1 tablespoon molasses

In a saucepan mix all ingredients, add baby carrots, bring to boil. Reduce heat to medium, leave pot uncovered, and continue cooking 20 to 25 minutes until carrots are tender. Place carrots in serving dish and drizzle with remaining liquid. Makes 4 to 6 servings.

Creamed Cucumbers

3 or 4 medium cucumbers, peeled and sliced
1 large onion, peeled and sliced into rings
1 tablespoon sugar
1/2 cup sour cream
1/2 cup salad dressing or mayonnaise
1/4 teaspoon dill
Salt and pepper to taste

Slice cucumbers and onion into a bowl. Mix other ingredients separately and whisk together. Pour over cucumbers and onions. Refrigerate for several hours. Makes 6 servings.

Creamy Mashed Potatoes

8 medium to large potatoes, peeled
1 stick butter or 1/2 cup or 8 tablespoons
Salt and pepper to taste
1 (12 ounce) can evaporated milk

Cover peeled potatoes with water and boil until tender. Drain. Add butter, salt and pepper, and enough evaporated milk until consistency you like. I always hand mash my potatoes. Serve. Makes 10 to 12 servings.

Cucumbers in Vinegar

2 to 3 medium sized cucumbers, peeled
1 medium onion, sliced
1/4 cup white vinegar (can add more or less)
3 or 4 cups water (enough to cover cucumbers in bowl)
1/2 teaspoon black pepper
1 teaspoon salt

Slice cucumbers in a bowl. Slice onions and break into rings. Add remaining ingredients. Refrigerate for several hours before serving. Will keep for several days in the fridge. Makes 4 servings.

Favorite Coleslaw

1 (14 ounce bag) precut cabbage or could shred up a half head of cabbage
1 small green pepper, chopped or grated
1 small onion, chopped or grated
1 medium carrot, shredded
1 1/2 teaspoons celery seed
1/2 teaspoon salt
4 tablespoons mayonnaise

Put shredded cabbage in large bowl. Add remaining ingredients and mayo. Mix well. Chill and serve. Makes about 8 servings.

Fresh Mustard and Turnip Greens

2 to 3 bunches of greens, about 2 pounds (can be turnip, mustard or collards)
1 large onion, chopped (optional)
1/2 cup chopped pork jowl
1 cup water
1 teaspoon sugar (optional)
2 to 3 slices bacon, cooked and crumbled on top (optional)

Bring water to a boil, add meat to pot and cook about five minutes. Remove stems from greens and wash several times. No need to drain greens. Add greens to pot along with onion and sugar. (Some people don't add sugar but I always add a small amount of sugar to fresh vegetables because I think it brings out the flavor. Cover greens and cook until tender. I cook mine about 15 minutes. I don't like them overcooked. Makes about 6 to 8 servings

Note: You can add more water. I like to have some pot likker on my greens.

Old Fashioned Ice Box Coleslaw

1/2 of a large head of cabbage or 1 small head chopped or grated
1 small purple onion, chopped (can use regular onion)
1 green pepper, chopped
1 carrot, chopped
1 teaspoon celery seeds
1 teaspoon salt
1/2 teaspoon black pepper
1/2 cup white granulated sugar
1/2 cup white vinegar
1/3 cup oil (I use Canola)
1 teaspoon dry mustard

Combine cabbage, onion, green pepper, carrot, celery seeds, salt and pepper in a large bowl. Set aside. Combine sugar, vinegar, oil and dry mustard in a saucepan and bring to a boil on top of the stove. Remove and let cool. Toss dressing with slaw mixture. Refrigerate several hours or overnight. Makes 7 to 8 cups coleslaw. Keeps up to a week refrigerated.

Roasted Potato Bites

6 to 8 medium potatoes, peeled and cut into chunks
4 tablespoons olive oil or Canola oil
1/2 teaspoon garlic powder (can use more)
1/2 teaspoon salt
1/4 teaspoon black pepper

Spray a large baking sheet. In a large bowl, combine potatoes and other ingredients. Stir well to make sure the potatoes are well coated. Spread out on baking pan. Bake in preheated 425 degree oven for 50 – 60 minutes, turning about 4 times while cooking. Makes 4 servings.

Note: You can use Italian seasoning, Parmesan cheese, dried leaf thyme or whatever seasonings you like in this dish.

Southern Baked Beans

2 (15 oz.) cans pork-n-beans, drained
1 small onion, chopped
1/2 cup brown sugar
1 tablespoon yellow mustard
1 tablespoon tomato ketchup
1 tablespoon molasses or dark syrup
2 slices bacon

Drain beans, combine with all other ingredients in an oven safe casserole dish. Place bacon slices on top. Cook uncovered in a preheated 350 degree over for 45 minutes. Makes 8 to 10 servings.

Note: You can make these beans in the crock pot, too. Just throw all ingredients in the crock pot and cook about 4 hours on low. If you cook a long time, the beans will get mushy.

Skillet Meals

Cheesy Sausage Tortellini Skillet

1 pound pork sausage
1 medium onion, chopped
1 medium green pepper, chopped
1 clove of garlic, chopped
1 teaspoon oregano
1 teaspoon dried basil
1/8 teaspoon black pepper
1/2 teaspoon salt
Pinch cayenne or a few drops hot sauce (optional)
1 (28 ounce) can crushed tomatoes in puree
1 (4 ounce) can green chilies, drained
3 cups refrigerated 3 cheese tortellini, uncooked
1 cup shredded mozzarella cheese
1/2 cup shredded cheddar cheese
Chopped fresh parsley for garnish (optional)

Brown the sausage with the onion, green pepper, garlic, oregano, basil, black pepper, salt and cayenne in a large skillet. Add the crushed tomatoes and green chilies. Add tortellini and stir well. Turn heat to simmer, cover skillet and let cook 25 minutes or until pasta is done. Remove skillet from heat, sprinkle on the mozzarella and cheddar cheese. Cover until cheese melts. Garnish with fresh parsley. Makes 8 to 10 servings.

Note: I use Brutoni Three Cheese Tortellini.

Okra and Potatoes Supreme

1 (12 ounce) bag frozen cut okra or about 1 1/2 cups fresh okra, chopped
5 slices bacon, cooked (save drippings)
1/2 cup chopped regular onion or green onion
6 potatoes, peeled and cubed
1/2 cup chopped green pepper
3/4 cup cornmeal
1 teaspoon salt
1 teaspoon black pepper
1 teaspoon garlic powder
1/4 teaspoon chili powder
3/4 to 1 cup oil (I use the leftover bacon drippings combined with Canola Oil
to make one cup)
Pinch cayenne
1/2 cup shredded cheddar cheese (optional)

Cook bacon, drain, crumble and set aside. Whisk together cornmeal, salt, black pepper, garlic powder, chili powder and cayenne. Combine okra, onion, potatoes, and green pepper and toss in cornmeal mixture. Heat oil in large skillet and fry okra and potato mixture until browned and potatoes are done. Remove and sprinkle on crumbled bacon with cheese if desired and serve. Makes 6 to 8 servings.

Spicy Shrimp Creole

1 pound fresh or frozen shrimp, peeled and deveined
1 cup chopped onion
1 cup chopped green pepper
1 cup chopped celery
4 tablespoons oil
1 (14.5) ounce can diced tomatoes
1 (8 ounce) can tomato sauce
1 (4 ounce) can green chilis, drained
1 teaspoon salt
1/2 teaspoon black pepper
1 teaspoon minced garlic
1/2 teaspoon cajun seasoning
1 tablespoon Worcestershire sauce
1 teaspoon chili powder
2 bay leaves
Several drops hot sauce

Cook onion, celery and green pepper in the oil until start to brown. Add diced tomatoes, tomato sauce, green chilies, salt, pepper, garlic, Cajun seasoning, Worcestershire sauce, chili powder, bay leaves and hot sauce. Simmer for about 30 minutes. Add shrimp to the skillet and cook another six to eight minutes until shrimp are done. Remove bay leaves. Makes 6 servings.

Beans and Franks with a Twist

2 (15 ounce) cans pork-n-beans, drained
1 (1 pound) package franks, cut up
3 tablespoons butter
1/2 cup chopped purple onion
1/2 cup chopped green pepper
1 (10 ounce) can diced tomatoes with green chilies, drained
1 tablespoon spicy brown mustard
1 teaspoon Worcestershire sauce
2 tablespoons molasses
1/3 cup brown sugar
1/2 teaspoon oregano
1/2 teaspoon salt
1/4 teaspoon black pepper
Shredded cheddar cheese (optional)

Melt the butter in a skillet on top of the stove. Brown green pepper, onions, and cut up franks. Add the drained pork-n-beans, drained diced tomatoes with green chilis, mustard, Worcestershire sauce, molasses, brown sugar, oregano, salt and pepper. Simmer about 20 minutes. Can sprinkle on shredded cheddar cheese either while still in the skillet or individual servings. Makes about 6 servings.

Note: You can use green onion or regular onion.

Cabbage, Bacon and Potato Skillet

5 to 6 slices bacon
3 tablespoons olive oil or leftover bacon drippings
4 carrots, scraped and thinly sliced
1 onion, peeled and chopped
1 teaspoon salt
1/2 teaspoon black pepper
1 teaspoon cumin
1 teaspoon turmeric
4 tablespoons butter (optional)
1/2 head cabbage, chopped or shredded
4 to 5 potatoes, peeled and cubed

Cook bacon, remove from skillet, drain and set aside. Saute onions and carrots until tender in bacon drippings or olive oil. Stir in butter, cabbage, salt, pepper, cumin, and turmeric. Cook uncovered about 20 minutes on medium heat stirring a couple times. Add potatoes, cover and simmer until potatoes are cooked or about another 20 minutes. Crumble bacon slices on top before serving. Makes 6 to 8 servings.

Cheesy Bacon and Cabbage Skillet

3 to 4 slices bacon, cooked and crumbled
1 tablespoon butter
2 tablespoons bacon drippings or oil (I use the drippings from the bacon)
1 small head cabbage, chopped (about 6 cups of chopped cabbage)
1/2 small onion, finely chopped
1/2 teaspoon black pepper
1 teaspoon salt
1 teaspoon minced garlic
1 teaspoon ground mustard
1 (4 ounce) jar pimentos, drained
4 ounces cream cheese, cut into small pieces
few drops hot sauce or pinch or cayenne (optional)

Cook bacon, drain, crumble and set aside. Melt butter in a large skillet, add bacon drippings or oil along with your chopped cabbage and onion. Sprinkle on black pepper, salt, minced garlic and ground mustard. Cook cabbage until tender and add pimentos, cream cheese and hot sauce. Cook until cream cheese is melted and stir in crumbled bacon. Makes 6 to 8 servings.

Note: You could use green pepper in place of the pimentos in this dish.

Cheesy Pepperoni Pizza Pasta Skillet

1 pound pork sausage, regular or hot
1 onion, chopped
1 green pepper, chopped
1/2 teaspoon salt
1/4 teaspoon black pepper
1/2 teaspoon garlic powder
1 teaspoon oregano or Italian seasoning
few drops hot sauce (optional)
1 (26 ounce) jar of your favorite pasta sauce
1 cup water
8 ounces penne pasta (can use any kind of pasta)
1 cup pepperoni slices
1 to 2 cups shredded mozzarella cheese

Brown sausage, onion and green paper. Drain. Add salt, pepper, garlic powder, oregano, hot sauce, pasta sauce and water. You can either cook your pasta ahead and add to the sausage or add it uncooked and simmer for about 20 minutes or until pasta is cooked. (If putting uncooked pasta in the skillet, cover your skillet while simmering) Sprinkle pepperoni slices on top along with the cheese. Simmer until pepperoni is hot and cheese is melted. Makes about 8 servings.

Cheesy Smoked Sausage Pasta Skillet

1 pound smoked sausage
2 tablespoons butter or margarine
1 medium onion, chopped
1 green pepper, chopped
1 teaspoon minced garlic
1/2 teaspoon salt
1/4 teaspoon black pepper
few drops hot sauce
1 (14.5 ounce) can chicken broth
1 (14.5 ounce) can diced tomatoes, undrained
1 (4 ounce) can green chilies, drained
2 1/2 cups uncooked rotini pasta (could use shells, macaroni, penne)
1 cup shredded cheese of your choice

Melt butter in skillet and brown sausage, onion and green pepper. Add garlic, salt, pepper, chicken broth, tomatoes, green chilies and pasta. Bring to a boil and let cook on low, uncovered, until pasta is tender about 20 minutes. Sprinkle on cheese while still hot. Makes 8 servings.

Note: You could also make this without the pasta and serve over rice for another easy and different dish.

Chicken Creole

4 to 6 chicken breasts (I use the frozen boneless, skinless ones) cut into inch size pieces
1/4 cup oil
1 medium onion, chopped
1 green pepper, chopped
1 cup chopped celery
1 (14.5 ounce) can petite diced tomatoes, undrained
1 cup chicken broth
1 (6 ounce) can tomato paste
1/4 teaspoon black pepper
1/2 teaspoon salt
1/2 teaspoon each dried basil, oregano, thyme, marjoram, and minced garlic
2 cups rice, cooked according to package directions

Saute chicken pieces in the oil until no longer pink. Remove and keep warm. In the same skillet, saute the onion, green pepper and celery in the remaining oil until tender. Stir in the tomatoes, broth, tomato paste and seasonings. Bring to a boil, reduce heat; cover and simmer for 5 minutes. Return chicken to the pan; heat through. Serve with rice. Makes about 8 servings.

Fried Cabbage with Sausage

1 stick butter or 1/2 cup or 8 tablespoons
1 small head of cabbage, chopped
1 small green pepper, chopped or cut into strips
1 small onion, chopped
1 pound polish sausage, sliced into round pieces (can use smoked sausage)
1 (15 ounce) can diced tomatoes
1/2 teaspoon salt
1/2 teaspoon black pepper
few drops of hot sauce (optional)

Melt butter in large skillet. Add cabbage, onion, and green pepper and cook on medium high for about 5 minutes stirring to keep from sticking to pan. Add remaining ingredients, cover and simmer for 20 – 25 minutes. Makes about 8 servings.

Fried Corn

8 ears fresh corn or 28 ounce package frozen corn
1 stick butter or margarine
2 tablespoons bacon drippings
1 tablespoon sugar
Salt to taste

Remove husks and silks from fresh corn, wash and cut corn off the cob. Scrape the cob to get out the juice. Melt butter in a large skillet, add fresh or frozen corn, bacon drippings and sugar. Cook on medium high heat until corn is done about 15 to 20 minutes. Add salt to taste. Makes 6 to 8 servings.

Note: You can add cooked crumbled bacon to the corn, too.

Hamburger Steak and Gravy

Steak Ingredients:
1 pound ground beef
1 egg
1/2 teaspoon salt
1/4 teaspoon black pepper
1/2 teaspoon garlic powder
1 teaspoon minced onion
1/2 cup quick-cooking oats
1/4 cup flour
2 tablespoons oil

Gravy Ingredients:
1 package onion soup mix
1 small onion, peeled and chopped
3 1/2 cups water
4 ounce can mushroom pieces, drained
Flour leftover from dredging steaks.

In a large mixing bowl combine ground beef, egg, salt, pepper, garlic powder, minced onion, oats. (I mix this up with my hands) Make into about 4 hamburger steaks and dredge in the 1/4 cup flour. Heat oil in skillet and brown steaks on both sides. Remove to a plate. Add the gravy "fixins" to your skillet, bring to a boil, stirring to mix well. Add steaks back to the skillet, turn heat to simmer and let cook about 30 to 35 minutes on low heat. Makes 4 steaks depending on size you make them.

Italian Sausage and Manwich Sandwich or Skillet Meal

1 pound Italian sausage
1 small green pepper, chopped
1/2 cup chopped green onion
1 tablespoon chopped fresh parsley or 1 teaspoon dried parsley
1 1/2 teaspoons dried basil
1/4 teaspoon black pepper
1/2 teaspoon salt
1/2 teaspoon minced garlic
1 (6.5 ounce) can sliced black olives, drained
1 (15 ounce) can original Manwich
1/2 cup shredded Parmesan cheese

Split and remove the casings on the Italian sausage. (I use a serrated knife to do this, works great) Combine the Italian sausage, green pepper, onion, parsley, basil, black pepper, salt and minced garlic in a skillet and cook until sausage is browned. Add olives and Manwich. Simmer about 15 or 20 minutes. Sprinkle on Parmesan cheese   Serve on buns or over rice. Makes about 8 servings.

Peach Mango Pork Chops and Rice

3 to 4 large pork chops
2 tablespoons oil
2 tablespoons all-purpose flour
2 cups chicken broth or a (14.5 ounce) can
1/2 cup peach mango preserves
1/2 teaspoon salt
1/4 teaspoon black pepper
2 tablespoons spicy brown mustard
2 teaspoons apple cider vinegar
1/4 cup brown sugar
1 1/4 cups rice, uncooked (I use instant rice, could use regular, too)

Brown the chops in the oil in a skillet on top of the stove. Remove the chops and set aside. Scrape the crumbs loose in the skillet and add the flour to the drippings like you were making a roux or gravy. Whisk together in a bowl the chicken broth, preserves, salt, pepper, mustard, cider vinegar and brown sugar. Mix this with your roux in the skillet. Add the pork chops back to the pan, cover and simmer for 10 to 12 minutes. Remove the chops and add the rice to the gravy. Simmer until rice is tender or about 10 minutes. Serve chops with rice. Makes 4 servings.

Pork Chop and Apple Skillet

6 pork chops
1/2 cup all-purpose flour
1/2 teaspoon garlic powder
1/2 teaspoon paprika
1/2 teaspoon salt
1/2 teaspoon black pepper
3 tablespoons cooking oil (I use Canola)
2 tablespoons butter or margarine
1 medium onion, chopped
2 large apples, cored and sliced with peeling left on
3/4 cup bottled honey barbecue sauce
1 teaspoon minced garlic
3/4 cup water

Place flour in a shallow dish. Mix in salt, pepper, paprika and garlic powder. Dredge chops in flour mixture, coating well. Add butter and oil to skillet and brown chops on both sides. Put chopped onion and apple slices on top of chops. In a bowl mix water, minced garlic and honey barbecue sauce with a whisk and pour over chops. Cover and simmer 35 – 40 minutes until pork chops are tender. Makes 6 servings.

Quick and Easy Hamburger Goulash

1 lb. ground beef
1 medium onion, chopped
1 (10 oz.) can tomato soup
1 (14 oz.) can diced tomatoes, undrained
1 tablespoon sugar
1 teaspoon minced garlic
1 teaspoon paprika
1 teaspoon apple cider vinegar
1/2 teaspoon salt
1/2 teaspoon black pepper
1 cup of water
1 teaspoon dried parsley flakes
1 teaspoon Italian seasoning or could use oregano
1 teaspoon Worcestershire sauce
2 cups Rotini pasta, uncooked

Cook ground beef and onion in a large skillet until beef is browned. Drain off grease from hamburger. Add soup, tomatoes and all other ingredients except pasta.
Cook until mixture starts to boil. Add pasta and simmer until it is tender, about 12 minutes. Makes 6 to 8 servings.

Note: Could top with cheese.

Sausage, Pasta and Cheese Skillet

1 small onion, chopped
1 pound package smoked sausage, sliced
2 tablespoons butter or margarine
1/2 teaspoon minced garlic
1 (14 ounce) can chicken broth
1/2 cup water
2 cups elbow macaroni, uncooked
8 ounces velveeta cheese, cubed, or your favorite cheese
1 (14 ounce) bag frozen garden blend vegetables
1/4 teaspoon black pepper
1/2 teaspoon salt

Melt butter in large skillet. Brown onion and sausage. Pour in chicken broth and and water and bring to a boil. Stir in macaroni and simmer about 10 minutes until pasta is tender. Add vegetables and stir. Sprinkle cheese over vegetables and cook about 10 to 12 minutes longer until cheese is melted and vegetables are tender stirring often. Makes 8 to 10 servings.

Note: For my frozen vegetables I use the broccoli, sugar snap peas, green beans, mushrooms, carrots, celery, onions and red peppers. You can use chicken, ham or polish sausage and any kind of pasta in this dish. Different vegetables as well.

Smoked Sausage, Tomatoes and Okra Skillet

1 (14 ounce) package smoked sausage, sliced in rounds
2 tablespoons bacon drippings or cooking oil
1 cup chopped green onion
1 chopped green pepper
3 cups peeled and chopped fresh tomatoes or 1 (14 ounce can diced tomatoes)
2 cups chopped fresh okra (could use frozen)
1 cup fresh or frozen corn (could use canned)
1 teaspoon salt
2 teaspoons brown sugar
1/2 teaspoon paprika
1 teaspoon minced garlic
1/2 teaspoon Cajun seasoning (optional)
few drops hot sauce

Brown sausage, green onion and green pepper in bacon drippings. Add all the remaining ingredients and simmer covered 15-20 minutes until okra is tender. Serve over rice. Makes 6 to 8 servings.

Note: You could add some fresh zucchini to this recipe, too. Just chop up a cup of zucchini and add when adding the vegetables.

Spanish Rice and Smoked Sausage

1 cup long-grain rice, uncooked
1 medium onion, chopped
1 small green pepper, chopped
1/2 cup celery, chopped
3 tablespoons butter
1 (14 ounce) can chicken broth
1 (7 ounce) can mushroom stems and pieces, drained
1 (14.5 ounce) can diced tomatoes, undrained
1/2 teaspoon minced garlic or 1 clove of garlic, chopped
1/2 teaspoon salt
1/2 teaspoon black pepper
1 lb. smoked sausage, sliced in rounds
dash hot sauce (optional)

Brown rice, onion, celery and green pepper in butter. Add broth, mushrooms, garlic, salt, pepper, tomatoes, sausage and hot sauce. Cover and let simmer for about 25 minutes until rice soaks up liquid. Makes about 6 to 8 servings.

Note: You could use turkey sausage, hamburger or turkey burger. If you use hamburger or turkey burger, you would brown it with the rice, onions, peppers and celery.

Sweet and Sour Pork Skillet

1 1/2 to 2 lbs. boneless pork, cut in chunks (can use boneless pork chops, tenderloin, ribs, or roast)
3 tablespoons oil (I use Canola)
1/2 teaspoon salt
1/4 teaspoon black pepper
1 medium onion, cut in rings
1 medium green pepper, cut in rings
1 (20 ounce) can pineapple chunks in juice
1/2 cup water
2 tablespoons apple cider vinegar
2 tablespoons soy sauce
1/2 cup brown sugar
2 tablespoons water
2 tablespoons cornstarch

Saute' pork, onions and green pepper in oil until pork is browned and onion and peppers are tender. Drain pineapple and reserve the juice. In a bowl mix juice from pineapple, 1/2 cup water, vinegar, soy sauce, brown sugar, salt and pepper. Pour over pork, onion and peppers in skillet. Cover and simmer about 20 minutes until meat is tender. In the same bowl mix cornstarch and 2 tablespoons water and beat with whisk until smooth. Add to pork in skillet. Cook on low, stirring constantly until mixture thickens. Add pineapple chunks and simmer about 5 minutes longer. Serve over rice. Makes 6 to 8 servings.

Zucchini Beef Skillet

1 pound ground beef
1 medium onion, chopped
1 green pepper, chopped
1 teaspoon garlic powder
1/2 teaspoon salt
1/2 teaspoon black pepper
1 teaspoon chili powder
2 fresh tomatoes, peeled and chopped
1 1/2 cups fresh or frozen corn
2 tablespoons pimiento
1 tablespoon dried parsley
5 cups unpeeled thinly sliced zucchini
1 package onion soup mix
3/4 cup water

Brown beef, onion and green pepper in a large skillet. Drain. Add remaining ingredients. Cover and simmer 15 to 20 minutes until vegetables are tender. Makes 8 to 10 servings.

Note: You don't have to peel the tomatoes unless you like them peeled. You can use yellow squash instead of zucchini or a mixture of both.

Beef Stoganoff

2 to 3 lb. round steak, cut in one inch cubes
Flour (about 1/2 a cup)
1 teaspoon salt
1/2 teaspoon black pepper
1/2 teaspoon garlic powder
3 tablespoons oil
3/4 to 1 cup water
1 teaspoon Worcestershire sauce
1 pint sour cream
1 (10 3/4 ounce) can cream of mushroom soup
Minute rice or noodles

Roll cubes of round steak in flour seasoned with salt, pepper, and garlic powder. Brown seasoned steak in 3 tablespoons canola oil on all sides. Add water and cook on low until meat is tender. Add 1 teaspoon Worcestershire sauce, 1 pint sour cream, and 1 can cream of mushroom soup. Simmer 10 to 15 minutes. Serve over rice or noodles. Makes 8 servings.

Fried Apples

4 or 5 apples, unpeeled, cored and sliced
2 tablespoons bacon drippings (optional)
2 tablespoons butter or margarine
2 tablespoons brown sugar
1 teaspoon cinnamon
1/2 teaspoon nutmeg
1 teaspoon salt

In a skillet over medium heat add bacon drippings and margarine. Add apple slices, brown sugar, cinnamon, nutmeg and salt. Stir well to make sure apples slices are covered with spices and brown sugar. Bring to a boil and cover. Cut heat back to simmer and cook for 20 – 25 minutes until apples are soft but not mushy. Remove from pan and spoon any remaining liquid over apples. Makes 6 servings.

Hamburger Creamed Gravy

1 pound ground beef
1/2 cup chopped onion
1 clove minced garlic
1/4 cup flour
1/2 teaspoon salt
1 teaspoon black pepper
1/2 teaspoon Worcestershire sauce
2 cups milk (I use one 12 ounce can of evaporated milk and enough water to make 2 cups)

Brown ground beef, onion and garlic until beef is cooked. Drain. Put hamburger back in skillet and add flour, salt, pepper, Worcestershire sauce and milk. Simmer until gravy thickens. Makes 6 to 8 servings.

Sausage and Rice Skillet Meal

1 lb pork sausage
1 green pepper, chopped
1 onion, peeled and chopped
1 cup chopped celery
1 (1 lb. can) mushroom stems and pieces, drained
1 can chicken broth
1 1/2 cups instant rice
1 (4 oz. can) diced green chili peppers (optional)
salt and pepper to taste

Brown sausage, with onion, green pepper, and celery in skillet. Drain. Add mushrooms, rice and chicken broth. Simmer until rice is tender. Makes 6 servings.

Slow Cooker Recipes

Cranberry Orange Pork Loin Roast

1 (3 to 4 pound) boneless pork loin roast
1 (14.5 ounce) can whole berry cranberry sauce
1 tablespoon spicy brown mustard
1 cup orange juice
1 teaspoon minced garlic
1/4 teaspoon black pepper
1/2 teaspoon salt
1/2 teaspoon dried thyme
2 tablespoons brown sugar

Trim excess fat from roast and brown on all sides in a skillet on top of the stove. Place roast in crock pot. Whisk together the cranberry sauce, mustard, orange juice, garlic, black pepper, salt, thyme and brown sugar until well mixed. Pour over the roast in the crock pot. Cook for 7 to 8 hours on low or 4 to 5 hours on high. Remove roast and slice or shred. You can thicken the gravy by adding a little cornstarch and heating to desired consistency on top of the stove or serve without thickening. I don't thicken my gravy. We make sandwiches from the leftovers. Makes about 8 servings depending on the size of your roast.

Barbecued Chicken Breast

2 – 4 boneless skinless chicken breasts
2/3 cup tomato ketchup
1 tablespoon apple cider vinegar
1/4 cup butter or margarine, melted
1/4 cup chopped onion
1 tablespoon brown sugar
1 tablespoon Dijon mustard
1 tablespoon Worcestershire sauce
1 tablespoon liquid smoke
1/4 teaspoon celery seeds
1/4 teaspoon minced garlic
1/4 teaspoon black pepper

Whisk all ingredients together in a bowl. Place chicken in crock pot and cover with sauce. Cook on low for 7 – 8 hours or high 4 – 5 hours. Makes 4 servings.

Note: This sauce could be used on pork as well as chicken. It gives both meats a great flavor.

Beef Stew

1 to 1 1/2 pounds of lean beef, chuck or stew meat, cut in bite-sized pieces
1/2 cup flour
3 tablespoons cooking oil or bacon drippings
3 or 4 carrots, cut in pieces
4 or 5 medium potatoes, peeled and cut in chunks
3 stalks of celery, cut in inch sized pieces
1 medium onion, peeled and cut in pieces
1 cup frozen peas (optional)
4 cups beef broth or 2 (14.5 ounce cans)
1 (14.5 ounce) can beef gravy
1/2 teaspoon salt
1 teaspoon black pepper
Pinch of cayenne
Few drops of hot sauce (optional)
3 tablespoons Worcestershire sauce
1/2 teaspoon garlic powder
1 (10 3/4 ounce) can cream of mushroom soup, undiluted
2 bay leaves

Dredge the stew meat in the flour and brown in oil on top of the stove. (Keep any leftover flour to thicken stew, if needed) Add meat to the crock pot along with carrots, potatoes, celery, onion and peas. Mix together beef broth, beef gravy, salt, pepper, cayenne, hot sauce, Worcestershire sauce, garlic powder and mushroom soup with a wire whisk. Pour over meat and vegetables in the crock pot, add bay leaves and cook on high 4 hours or low 8 hours or until vegetables are done. (If you want a thicker gravy remove some of the liquid about 25 minutes before serving, add a couple tablespoons of the leftover flour from dredging the meat and return to the crock pot to thicken the gravy). Remove bay leaves.   Makes 8 to 10 servings.

Beer Brats and Sauerkraut

1 (14 ounce) package Johnsonville Smoked Brats
1 (2 pound) bag sauerkraut, rinsed and drained
1 onion, sliced and separated in rings
1 green pepper, cut in rings
1 (12 ounce) beer
1 tablespoon Dijon mustard
1/4 cup apple juice
1/4 cup brown sugar
1 teaspoon caraway seeds
1 teaspoon thyme
1 bay leaf

Place sauerkraut in bottom of crock pot with onion and green pepper on top. Whisk together the beer, mustard, apple juice, caraway seeds, thyme and brown sugar. Pour over the sauerkraut, green pepper and onion. Add bay leaf to pot. Place brats on top and cook on high for 4 hours or low for 6 hours until peppers, onions and brats are well done. Remove bay leaf. Serve brats on hoagie buns covered with sauerkraut, peppers and onions. Makes 8 to 10 brats.

Cajun Beef Roast

1 (3 or 4 lb.) chuck roast
1 green pepper, chopped
1 cup chopped celery
1 (14.5 ounce) can diced tomatoes
1 (4 ounce) can green chilis
1/4 cup quick-cooking tapioca
1 large onion, peeled, sliced in rings
1 cup chopped okra (optional)
1/4 teaspoon black pepper
1/4 teaspoon cayenne (can use more or less)
1/4 teaspoon onion powder
1/2 teaspoon garlic powder
1/4 teaspoon thyme
1/4 teaspoon chili powder
1/2 teaspoon basil
1 bay leaf
1 cup water

Cut roast to fit into crock pot and place in bottom. In a large bowl combine the remaining ingredients and mix with a spoon. Pour over the roast. Cook on high for about 5 hours or low 7 until meat is tender. Serve over rice. Makes a 3 quart crock pot 3/4 full.

Note: The tapioca acts as a thickening agent in the recipe. You can leave it out if you want a more soupy gravy.

Chicken, Broccoli and Pasta

4 or 5 boneless chicken breasts
1/4 cup all-purpose flour
1/2 teaspoon salt
1/2 teaspoon black pepper
1/2 teaspoon garlic powder
1 (10 3/4 ounce) can cream of broccoli soup
1 (10 3/4 ounce) can cream of chicken soup
1/2 soup can of water
1 (7 ounce) can mushroom stems and pieces, undrained
1 small onion, chopped
1 lb. bag of baby carrots (I cut them in half)
1 lb. bag of frozen broccoli cuts
2 bay leaves
1 1/2 cups penne pasta or pasta of choice
3/4 cup shredded sharp cheddar cheese

In a shallow dish combine flour, salt, pepper, and garlic powder. Cover chicken pieces with mixture and rub into chicken. Place chicken pieces in slow cooker and pour any flour mixture that is left over the chicken. In a bowl combine soups, water, mushrooms, onion, carrots and broccoli cuts. Mix and pour over the chicken. Add bay leaves. Cover and cook on high 4 to 5 hours or low for 6 to 7 hours. About 40 minutes before recipe is done add the pasta and cheese. Makes 6 servings.

Note: You could cut the chicken in strips.

Chicken, Potatoes and Broccoli

3 or 4 chicken breasts, not frozen
3 or 4 medium potatoes, peeled and cut into chunks
1 medium onion, peeled and sliced in rings
1 package onion soup mix
1 (10 3/4 ounce) can cream of mushroom soup
1 cup milk
1 (4 ounce) can mushrooms, undrained
1/2 teaspoon black pepper
1/2 teaspoon parsley flakes
1/2 teaspoon basil
1 bay leaf
1 teaspoon salt
1 (1 pound) bag frozen broccoli cuts

Add chicken to crock pot, whisk remaining ingredients together in a bowl except broccoli, pour over chicken pieces. Cook on high for 4 hours or low 7 to 8 hours. About 30 minutes before serving add the broccoli to the crock pot and cook until tender. Serves 4 to 6 depending on number of chicken pieces.

Coca Cola Pork Chops

4 to 6 pork chops (I use bone-in, center cut chops but any pork chops will do)
1 cup coca cola (can use diet coke, pepsi, or any cola drink)
2 tablespoons brown sugar
1/4 teaspoon black pepper
1/2 teaspoon salt
1 cup ketchup
1 cup chopped onion
2 tablespoons grape jelly (optional)
1 teaspoon minced garlic

Brown chops in skillet on top of the stove. Place in crock pot. Whisk together the coke, brown sugar, black pepper, salt, ketchup, chopped onion, jelly and minced garlic with a wire whisk. Pour over chops. Cook 7 to 8 hours on low or 4 to 5 hours on high. Serve chops with the gravy poured over them. Makes 4 to 6 servings.

Note: These chops are so tender they just fall apart. You could double or triple this recipe and pour over just about any pork roast or ribs.

Corned Beef and Cabbage

3 to 4 pound corned beef brisket
5 carrots
5 potatoes, peeled and cut in chunks
1 medium head cabbage, cut in wedges
1 medium onion, peeled and cut up
4 bay leaves
1 teaspoon minced garlic
1 (14.5 ounce) can chicken broth
1 (12 ounce) can beer
2 tablespoons butter or margarine, melted
1/2 cup water
Seasoning packet that comes with brisket
1/2 teaspoon black pepper

Put brisket in the bottom of the crock pot and add potatoes, carrots, onion and cabbage on top. Mix together remaining ingredients and pour over brisket and vegetables. Cook on low 7 or 8 hours or high about 5 hours. This makes a five quart crock pot about 3/4 full.

Note: If you don't want to use alcohol you can add extra chicken broth.

Country Style Ribs

3 – 4 lbs. pork coountry style ribs
1 small onion, chopped
1 teaspoon cajun seasoning
1/2 teaspoon black pepper
1/2 cup tomato ketchup
2 tablespoons maple syrup or sorghum molasses
1 tablespoon Worcestershire sauce
2 teaspoons Dijon mustard
1 teaspoon cinnamon
1 teaspoon minced garlic
1/2 teaspoon allspice
2 tablespoons brown sugar
1/2 teaspoon salt

Place ribs in crock pot. In a bowl mix all the other ingredients together and pour over ribs. Cook on high for 4 hrs. or low for 6 to 7 hours until ribs are tender. Place ribs on a platter and spoon on remainder of sauce. Makes approximately 8 servings.

Dijon Chicken Breast

4 to 6 chicken breasts, not frozen
1 (10 3/4 ounce) can Campbells Cream of Chicken Soup, undiluted
2 tablespoons Dijon mustard
1 1/2 cups water
1 package Lipton Onion Soup Mix
1/4 teaspoon salt
1/8 teaspoon black pepper
1/4 teaspoon dried basil
1/4 teaspoon parsley flakes
1/4 teaspoon garlic powder
1 (4 ounce) can mushrooms, drained
2 tablespoons cornstarch
Noodles or rice

Place chicken breasts in crock pot. Mix all the other ingredients together in a bowl except cornstarch and noodles or rice. Mix together with a spoon and pour over chicken breasts. Cook on low for 6 to 7 hours or high for 4 to 5 hours until chicken is done. Remove chicken from crock pot. Take 1 cup of the liquid out and whisk the cornstarch into the liquid and add back to the crock pot. Turn pot to high for about 15 minutes and remove lid to let gravy thicken   Prepare noodles according to package directions. Once noodles are cooked, add them to the gravy in the crock pot and mix together. Remove from pot and serve with chicken breasts. You could also serve this over rice. Makes 4 to 6 servings.

Fiesta Chicken

4 to 6 boneless, skinless chicken breasts
1 (1.5 ounce) package of taco seasoning mix
1/4 teaspoon cumin
1/4 teaspoon garlic powder
1/4 teaspoon chili powder
1/4 teaspoon black pepper
pinch of cayenne pepper (optional)
1 cup picante sauce
1 small green pepper, chopped
1 small onion, chopped
1 (14.5 ounce) can diced tomatoes with roasted onion and garlic, drained (can use diced tomatoes with green chilies)
Sour cream
Shredded cheese

The night before you put this in the crock pot combine the taco seasoning, cumin, garlic powder, black pepper and cayenne in a bowl and mix well. Put the chicken breasts in a large plastic ziploc bag (I use a gallon sized bag and you can put the chicken in the bag frozen) and dump in the seasonings. Shake well to cover the chicken with the mixture. Put in the refrigerator overnight. The next morning place chicken breasts in crock pot and pour in extra seasoning mix over them. Add the chopped green pepper, onion, picante sauce, and diced tomatoes over the chicken. Cook on high for 4 – 5 hours or low for 7 – 8 hours. Serve with sour cream and shredded cheese. Makes 4 to 6 servings.

Hamburger and Beans Supreme

1 1/2 to 2 pounds ground beef
1 large onion, chopped
1 small green pepper, chopped
1 clove of garlic, chopped
1 (16 ounce) can pork-n-beans, drained
1 (15.5 ounce) can kidney beans, drained
1 (15.5 ounce) can red beans, drained
1 (10 ounce) can diced tomatoes with green chilies, undrained
1 (10 3/4 ounce) can tomato soup, undiluted
1 teaspoon salt
1/2 teaspoon black pepper
Pinch cayenne or several drops hot sauce (optional)
1 tablespoon Worcestershire sauce
1 (4 ounce) can mushroom pieces, drained
1 teaspoon liquid smoke (optional)

Brown ground beef, onion, green pepper and garlic in skillet on top of the stove. Drain. Add to crock pot along with remaining ingredients. Cook on low for about 4 hours until flavors have blended. Makes a 3 quart crock pot about three fourths full. Serve with toppings of your choice.

Homemade Applesauce

10 medium sized apples, peeled and cored, cut up in pieces
1 cup water
1/2 cup brown sugar
2 teaspoons ground cinnamon
1/2 teaspoon ground nutmeg
1/4 teaspoon ground allspice
1/4 teaspoon cardamom
2 to 3 tablespoons honey

Place apples in crock pot. Mix together water, brown sugar, cinnamon, nutmeg, allspice, cardamom and honey with a wire whisk. Pour over apples. Cook on low for 7 to 8 hours or high 4 hours. Great as a side dish for any meal. Will keep at least two weeks or longer in the fridge. Makes about 1 1/2 quarts

Note: You can mash up the apples in the cooked sauce if you want to make it smoother.

Note: I used Red Delicious for this one but you could use about any kind of apple.

Honey Soy Pork Chops

4 to 6 pork chops (I use bone-in center cut but you could use any chops)
1/2 cup flour
1 tablespoon Montreal Steak Seasoning (optional)
1/2 teaspoon black pepper
4 tablespoons cooking oil
1 green pepper, seeded and sliced
1 medium onion, peeled and sliced in rings
1 (14.5 ounce) can diced tomatoes, undrained
1/2 cup water
1/3 cup honey or 1/2 cup brown sugar
1/3 cup soy sauce

Combine flour, steak seasoning and pepper in a brown bag or shallow pan. Cover chops with flour. Brown in oil on top of the stove. Place pork chops in crock pot with sliced green pepper and onion rings on top. Combine tomatoes, water, honey and soy sauce and pour over the top. Cook on low 6 to 7 hours or high 3 to 4 hours. Makes 4 to 6 servings.

Note: I don't add salt to this recipe because the soy sauce makes it salty enough for us. You can add more salt if you want.

Italian Sausage Spaghetti

1 to 1 1/2 pounds Italian sausage
1 tablespoon olive oil or cooking oil
3 green peppers, seeded and cut into rings.
1 large onion, peeled and cut into rings
1 (10 ounce) can tomatoes and green chilies
1 (8 ounce) can tomato sauce
1 (14.5 ounce) can chicken broth
1 teaspoon oregano or Italian seasoning
1 teaspoon minced garlic
1 teaspoon dried basil
1 bay leaf
1/4 teaspoon black pepper
1/2 teaspoon salt
Few drops hot sauce (optional)
8 ounces thin or angel hair pasta

Brown the Italian sausage in a skillet on top of the stove in the oil. Add the pepper and onion rings to the crock pot and place browned Italian sausage on top. In a large bowl combine the tomatoes and green chilies, tomato sauce, chicken broth, oregano, garlic, basil, bay leaf, black pepper, salt and hot sauce. Stir to combine. Pour over the sausage, onions and peppers. Cook on low heat in the crock pot 7 to 8 hours or high 4 to 5 hours. Remove sausage from pot and set aside. Turn the temperature to high on the crock pot and add the spaghetti for about 30 minutes until tender and cooked. (I use the thin or angel hair because it cooks in 30 minutes. If you use the thick it will take a little longer). Remove bay leaf before serving. You can add the sausage back to the pot if you want to reheat it or just serve over the spaghetti and peppers on a platter. Makes 6 to 8 servings.

Juicy Beef Roast

1 (4 or 5 pound) chuck roast
1/4 cup apple cider vinegar
1 (8 ounce) can tomato sauce
1/4 cup brown sugar
1 teaspoon liquid smoke
1 teaspoon Worcestershire sauce
1/2 teaspoon ground cinnamon
1 teaspoon Dijon mustard
1/2 teaspoon minced garlic
1/2 teaspoon chili powder
1/2 teaspoon salt
1/2 teaspoon black pepper
1 teaspoon hot sauce (optional)

Put all ingredients in a bowl and whisk together until sauce is well blended and smooth. Pour over roast in crock pot. Cook on high for 4 or 5 hours or low for seven to eight hours.   Serve as main dish with sauce drizzled over meat. Makes 8 to 10 servings.

Picante Chicken

3 to 4 boneless, skinless chicken breasts
1/4 cup picante sauce
1 small onion, chopped
1 (10 ounce) can diced tomatoes and green chilies
2 tablespoons brown sugar
1/2 teaspoon dried cilantro
1 teaspoon minced garlic
1 (10.5 ounce) can cream of mushroom soup
1 cup chopped green and red peppers
few drops hot sauce
1/2 teaspoon salt
1/2 teaspoon black pepper

Place chicken pieces in bottom of crock pot. Mix together remaining ingredients and pour over chicken. Cook 6 to 7 hours on low until chicken is done or 3 to 4 hours on high. Makes 4 servings depending on amount of chicken you use.

Note: You could use any part of the chicken for this recipe.

Polish Sausage, Sauerkraut and Potatoes

2 (14 ounce) cans sauerkraut, undrained (or 1 (2 pound) bag)
5 or 6 potatoes, peeled and cut into large chunks
1 cup water
1 pound Polish sausage, cut into chunks (could use smoked sausage)
1 teaspoon caraway seeds
1 bay leaf
1/4 teaspoon black pepper

Place sauerkraut and potatoes in crock pot, add spices and water. Place sausage on top. Cook 4 hours on high or about 6 hours on low or until potatoes are done. Makes 6 to 8 serving.

Pork Roast and White Beans

3 to 4 pound pork roast
1 pound bag dried Great Northern white beans
1 small onion, chopped (optional)
Salt and pepper to taste
1 teaspoon minced garlic

Soak beans overnight according to package directions, drain. Next morning, add roast and beans to crock pot, along with chopped onion, garlic and pepper. (I don't salt my beans until they are done). Add enough water to cover beans and leave a little space at the top or crock pot will run over when it starts to boil. Cook on high for 4 to 5 hours or low 7 to 8 hours until done. Makes approximately 8 to 10 servings.

Pulled Pork Barbecue

1 (5 pound) Boston butte pork roast
1/2 cup water
1 teaspoon salt
1/2 teaspoon black pepper
1 1/2 cups finely chopped onion
1 teaspoon minced garlic
1/4 cup apple cider vinegar
1/2 teaspoon liquid smoke
1/2 cup tomato ketchup
1/3 cup brown sugar
1 teaspoon Worcestershire sauce
3 or 4 drops tabasco (could use more)
1/4 cup honey
1/2 teaspoon cumin

Place pork roast in crock pot with 1/2 cup water, salt and pepper. Cook on low for 6 to 7 hours until roast is tender or high for 4 hours. Remove roast and drain off liquids. (Reserve some of the liquid) Shred roast with a fork and put back in crock pot. Mix remaining ingredients together in a bowl with a wire whisk along with 1/2 cup of drained pork juices. Pour over roast and cook for at least 2 more hours in crock pot on low. Roast should be wet but not soupy. If it looks too dry add a little more of the juice you drained off. This can be done with beef roast, too. Makes 10 to 12 servings and keeps well in the fridge for 4 to 5 days.

Pumpkin Chili

1 to 1 1/2 pounds ground beef
1 onion, peeled and chopped
1 green pepper, chopped
1 (15 ounce) can 100% pure pumpkin
1 (10 ounce) can tomatoes and green chilis
1 (15.5 ounce) can chili beans, undrained
1 (15 ounce) can black beans, undrained
1 (14.5 ounce) can diced tomatoes, undrained
1/2 cup water
1/2 teaspoon minced garlic
1 teaspoon ground cinnamon
1/2 teaspoon ginger
1/4 teaspoon allspice
1/4 teaspoon nutmeg
2 teaspoons chili powder
1/2 teaspoon salt
1/4 teaspoon black pepper

Brown your ground beef, onion and green pepper in a skillet. Drain. Add all ingredients to crock pot and cook on high for about 3 hours or low 6 hours. Be sure to check to see if you need to add more water. Makes 10 to 12 servings.

Serve with a dollop of sour cream and your favorite shredded cheese on top.

Round Steak and Gravy

2 to 3 lb. round steak, cut in serving size pieces
1 stick butter or 1/2 cup or 8 tablespoons
1/2 cup all-purpose flour
1 teaspoon garlic powder
1/2 teaspoon salt
1/2 teaspoon black pepper
1 medium sized onion, peeled and sliced
1 package onion soup mix
1 (14.5 oz) can beef broth
2 (7 oz.) cans mushrooms, drained (optional)
1 teaspoon brown sugar
1/4 teaspoon ground allspice
1/2 teaspoon ground ginger
1 bay leaf
3 to 4 carrots, scraped and cut in pieces

In a bowl combine flour, garlic powder, salt and pepper. Coat steak pieces with flour mixture. Melt butter in skillet and brown steak on both sides. Remove steak and put in crock pot. Cover steak pieces with the sliced onion broken into onion rings. Add carrots. In a bowl whisk together the onion soup mix, beef broth, mushrooms, brown sugar, allspice, and ginger. (If you have any leftover flour from dredging meat you can add this to the broth, too) Pour over steak, onion and carrots. Add bay leaf. Cook on high for 5 to 6 hours or low for 8 to 9 hours or until meat is tender. Remove bay leaf before serving. Great over rice, noodles or mashed potatoes. Makes 6 to 8 servings.

Santa Fe Stew

1 1/2 pounds ground beef
1 small onion, chopped
1 small green pepper, chopped
1/2 teaspoon minced garlic
1/2 teaspoon black pepper
1/2 teaspoon cumin
1 teaspoon salt
1 (15 ounce) can pinto beans, undrained
1 (15 ounce) can black beans, undrained
1 (15 ounce) can kidney beans, undrained
1 (15 ounce) can whole kernel white sweet corn, drained
1 (14.5 ounce) can petite diced tomatoes, undrained
1 (4 ounce) can chopped green chilies
1 (1.5 ounce) package taco seasoning
1 (1 ounce) package ranch dressing mix

Brown ground beef with onion, green pepper and spices in a skillet on top of the stove. Add all ingredients to crock pot and mix in ground beef mixture. Cook on low 2 to 3 hours. This makes a 3 quart crock pot almost full to the top, approximately 10 to 12 servings.

Sausage and Veggies with Peppers

1 pound smoked sausage, cut in pieces
6 potatoes, peeled and halved
1 large onion, peeled and sliced or chopped
3 or 4 large carrots, scraped and cut in pieces
1 large green pepper, seeded and chopped
1 large red sweet pepper, seeded and chopped
1 (14 ounce) can beef broth or 2 cups
1 package onion soup mix
2 bay leaves
1 teaspoon basil
1 teaspoon minced garlic
1/2 teaspoon black pepper
1 teaspoon Worcestershire sauce

Place sausage and vegetables in crock pot. Mix together the broth, onion soup, spices and Worcestershire sauce and pour over the vegetables. Cook on low for 5 or 6 hours or high for 3 to 4 hours until the potatoes and carrots are done. Makes 6 to 8 servings.

Sausage, White Bean and Pasta Soup

1 pound breakfast pork sausage (can use mild or hot, I use the mild)
1 small onion, chopped
1 tablespoon dried basil
1 teaspoon minced garlic
1 (14.5 ounce) can chicken broth
1 (14.5 ounce) can diced tomatoes, undrained
1 1/2 cups water
1 (8 ounce) can tomato sauce
1 (10 3/4 ounce) can cream of celery soup
1/2 package baby carrots or 3 to 4 carrots cut in pieces
1 cup dried great northern beans
1/2 cup elbow macaroni or pasta shells
1 tablespoon black pepper
Salt to taste
1/2 cup cabbage, shredded (optional)

Brown sausage and onion with basil and garlic in a skillet. Drain and pour into crock pot. Add all other ingredients except the pasta. Cook on low for seven to eight hours or high for 4 or 5 hours. About an hour before soup finishes cooking, add pasta. This could be made on top of the stove as well. Just cook in large pot until beans are tender. Then add pasta or shells about the last 20 minutes. Makes about 3 quarts of soup.

Smoked Sausage Gumbo

1 (1 lb.) package smoked sausage (beef or turkey) sliced in small pieces.
1 (14.5 ounce) can diced tomatoes
1/2 cup chopped celery
1 small green pepper, chopped
1 small onion, chopped
1 (1 lb.) package frozen chopped okra
1 (14.5 ounce can) can chicken broth
3 tablespoons olive oil
2 1/2 cups water
1/2 cup minute rice (white or brown)
1 teaspoon pepper (regular or cayenne)
1 teaspoon dry mustard
1 teaspoon paprika
1 teaspoon ground sage
1 teaspoon cumin
1 teaspoon thyme
1 teaspoon parsley flakes
2 bay leaves

Brown sausage, onion, and green pepper in olive oil and add to crock pot along with the rest of the ingredients. Cook on high for four hours or low for six hours. This is a hearty and filling soup. Makes about 3 quarts.

Spicy Pork Loin Roast

1 (2 -3 pound) pork loin roast
1/4 cup brown sugar
1/4 cup ketchup
2 teaspoons minced garlic
1/4 teaspoon black pepper
1/2 teaspoon salt
1/2 cup chopped green onions
1 tablespoon spicy brown mustard
1 tablespoon apple cider vinegar
1 tablespoon Worcestershire sauce
1/3 cup water
several drops hot sauce or pinch of cayenne
1/4 cup butter or 4 tablespoons, melted

Place your pork loin in the crock pot. Whisk together all the remaining ingredients and pour over pork loin. Cook on low for 7 to 8 hours or high for 4 to 5. Serve sauce from pot over meat and garnish with extra chopped green onions. Makes 6 to 8 servings depending on size of your tenderloin.

Sweet Potatoes, Pineapple and Cranberries

3 large sweet potatoes, peeled and cubed
1 1/2 cups fresh cranberries (could use frozen)
1 medium apple, peeled and chopped
1 teaspoon ground cinnamon
1/2 teaspoon ground nutmeg
1 cup brown sugar
1 (20 ounce) can pineapple chunks, drained (reserve 1/2 cup of the pineapple juice)
2 tablespoons butter
1 cup walnuts or pecans, toasted

Place sweet potatoes, cranberries and apple in crock pot. In a bowl whisk together the ground cinnamon, nutmeg, brown sugar and 1/2 cup of reserved pineapple juice. Pour over the sweet potatoes, cranberries and apple. Toss to cover well. Add butter to crock pot. Place drained pineapple chunks in refrigerator to add later. Cook on low for 6 to 7 hours or high for 4 hours. Stir to cover with juices a couple times. About an hour before recipe is done, add the drained pineapple and toss with juices to cover. Toast nuts by placing a single layer of nuts on a microwave-safe plate and nuke them for 1-minute intervals until they become crunchy. Sprinkle on top of your dish before serving. Makes about 6 to 8 servings.

Zesty Chicken

1 whole chicken (can remove skin, optional)
1/2 cup chicken broth or 1 chicken bouillon cube dissolved in 1/2 cup boiling water
1/3 cup soy sauce
1/4 cup olive oil
1/4 cup honey
1 teaspoon Worcestershire sauce
2 teaspoons balsamic vinegar
1 teaspoon sesame oil (optional)
2 teaspoons lemon juice
2 tablespoons minced garlic

Wash chicken and empty cavity. Remove skin if desired. Pat chicken dry and place breast down in slow cooker. In a bowl whisk together all the ingredients and pour over chicken. Cook on high for 4 hours or low for 8 hours. Spoon sauce over cooked chicken before serving.

Apricot Ribs

2 to 3 pounds pork ribs
1/2 cup apricot preserves
1 tablespoon tomato ketchup
2 tablespoons apple cider vinegar
2 tablespoons soy sauce
3 tablespoons brown sugar
1/2 teaspoon chili powder
1/2 teaspoon cumin
1/4 teaspoon black pepper
1/4 teaspoon cinnamon
1/4 teaspoon garlic powder
1 teaspoon minced onion

Place ribs in bottom of crock pot. Whisk together the rest of the ingredients in a bowl and pour over the ribs. Cook on low six to seven hours or high 4 to 5 until ribs are tender. Makes about 4 servings depending on how many ribs you use.

Beef and Tomato Gravy

1 (3 to 5 lb.) chuck roast or roast of your choice
2 (8 ounce) cans tomato sauce
1 teaspoon liquid smoke
1 teaspoon minced garlic
1 teaspoon worcestershire sauce
1/2 cup chopped onion
1 teaspoons sugar
1 tablespoon horseradish sauce
1/2 teaspoon black pepper
1/2 teaspoon salt
1/2 teaspoon thyme
1/4 teaspoon dried oregano
1/2 teaspoon dried parsley

Place roast in crock pot. Whisk together the tomato sauce and spices and pour over the roast. Cook on high 4 or 5 hours or low for 7 to 8 hours until roast is tender. Makes 8 to 10 servings.

Cabbage and Ham

4 or 5 potatoes, peeled and cut into chunks
1 cup chopped celery
1 medium onion, chopped
3 cups ham, cooked and cut into chunks
1/2 head cabbage, shredded or chopped
1 (1 pound) bag baby carrots (can use regular carrots)
1/2 teaspoon black pepper
1 large bay leaf
1/2 teaspoon celery seeds
1/2 teaspoon minced garlic
1 teaspoon salt
2 (14 ounce) cans chicken broth

Add all the ingredients to the crock pot. Cover with the chicken broth. Cook on high for 4 hours or low for 8 hours. Remove bay leaf and serve. Makes 8 to 10 servings.

Cabbage, Potatoes and Smoke Sausage

1/2 head cabbage cut into chunks
5 or 6 potatoes peeled and cut into chunks
1 lb. smoked sausage cut into pieces
Salt and pepper to taste
Enough water to fill slow cooker half full

Add all ingredients to crock pot, cook on high for about 4 hours or low for about six hours until potatoes are done. Makes 6 to 8 servings.

Chicken, Apple, Potatoes and Cabbage

3 or 4 boneless, skinless chicken breasts, cut in thirds
1/2 head cabbage shredded
1 onion, peeled and separated in rings
2 (15 oz.) cans chicken broth
4 or 5 medium potatoes, peeled and cut into chunks
2 or 3 small apples, peeled, cored and sliced
3 tablespoons soy sauce
1 teaspoon ginger
Dash red pepper or several drops hot pepper sauce
Salt and Pepper

Place shredded cabbage in bottom of crock pot. Add onion rings, apple slices, and chicken pieces. Add salt and pepper and hot sauce to chicken pieces. Place potatoes on top of chicken. Add soy sauce and ginger to chicken broth and pour into crock pot. Cook 7 hours on low. If liquid gets low add some water. Makes 6 to 8 servings.

Cranberry Chicken

2 or 3 boneless, skinless chicken breasts
1 (14 ounce) can whole cranberry sauce
1 envelope dry onion soup mix
1/2 cup water
2 tablespoons quick cooking tapioca (optional)
2 tablespoons brown sugar

Place chicken in crock pot. Combine all the ingredients, mix well, pour over chicken, cook for 4 hours on high or 6 to 8 hours on low. Spoon sauce over chicken before serving. Makes 4 to 6 servings.

Note: You could use legs or thighs or a whole chicken in this recipe.

Ham and Potatoes

6 to 8 slices of ham, chopped
4 or 5 potatoes, peeled and sliced
1 medium onion, chopped
1 cup grated cheese of your choice
1 can cream of mushroom soup, undiluted
Salt and pepper to taste

Start with a layer of potatoes, ham, onion, salt and pepper and cheese. Continue until all ingredients are in crock pot. Pour a can of cream of mushroom soup over the top. Cook on low 6 or 7 hours until potatoes are cooked. If needed add a little water after about 4 hours to keep potatoes from sticking to pot. Makes 6 to 8 servings.

Manwich Chicken

2 to 4 chicken breasts, uncooked
1 (15.5 ounce) can Manwich Original Sloppy Joe Sauce
1/4 cup salsa
3 to 4 tablespoons honey (optional)
1 small onion, chopped
1 small green pepper, chopped

Place chicken breasts in bottom of the crock pot. Mix remaining ingredients and pour over the chicken. Cook on high for 4 to 5 hours or low for 7 hours. Makes 4 servings.

Note: You can use frozen, fresh or any other pieces of chicken in this recipe.

Pork Roast and Sauerkraut

2 – 3 lb. pork roast
2 lb. bag of sauerkraut, undrained
 cup apple juice
1 small onion, chopped
1 cup water
1 pkg. dry onion soup mix
1/3 cup brown sugar
Salt and pepper

Sprinkle pork roast with salt and pepper and place in crock pot. (Cut to fit pot if roast is too big) In a large bowl, mix the rest of the ingredients together with a spoon. Pour the mixture over the roast. Cook on high for 4 hours or low for 8 hours until meat is cooked and tender. Remove roast and pull apart. Remove kraut with a slotted spoon. Makes approximately 6 to 8 servings.

Roast Beef and Vegetables

1 medium sized roast of your choice.
6 or 7 potatoes, peeled and cut up
5 or 6 carrots, sliced
1 large onion, peeled and chopped
2 cans cream of mushroom soup, undiluted
2 packages dry onion soup mix
1/2 teaspoon of salt
1/2 teaspoon of black pepper

Add roast, potatoes, carrots, and onions to crock pot. Mix dry onion soup with cream of mushroom soup, salt and pepper and pour over the meat and vegetables. Cook seven hours on low heat or until vegetables and meat are tender. Makes 8 to 10 servings depending on roast size.

Note: I usually use a chuck roast for this recipe.

Round Steak with Peppers and Onions

1 (2 to 3 lb.) round steak, cut in serving size pieces
1/2 to 1 cup all-purpose flour
1 teaspoon black pepper
1 teaspoon salt
1 teaspoon Oregano or Italian seasoning
1 teaspoon garlic powder
1/4 cup oil
1 large onion, peeled and seeded and cut in rings
2 green peppers, cut in rings (can use red or orange, I use all three)
2 (14.5 oz) cans diced tomatoes

Cut round steak in serving size pieces. Roll in flour that has been seasoned with the pepper, salt, oregano and garlic powder. Brown in oil on each side. You don't completely cook the meat just brown it good. Place browned meat in crock pot and put the rest of the ingredients on top of the meat. Cook on high for 4 hours or low for about 6 hours. Makes 6 to 8 servings.

Spicy Apricot Chicken

4 boneless, skinless chicken breasts, fresh or frozen
1 teaspoon salt
1/2 teaspoon coarse ground black pepper (can use regular ground black pepper)
1 cup Apricot preserves
1/2 cup honey
1 package dry onion soup mix
1/4 teaspoon ginger
1/4 teaspoon ground cloves
1 teaspoon Dijon mustard

Rub salt and pepper into chicken breasts and place into crock pot. Mix together remaining ingredients in a bowl and pour over chicken. Cook on high for 4 hours or low for 6 hours. Serve over rice. Makes 4 to 6 servings.

Stew Meat and Lima Beans

2 lbs. beef stew meat
1 teaspoon black pepper
1 teaspoon salt
1/2 teaspoon garlic powder
2 (12 ounce) pkgs. frozen lima beans
1 (14 ounce) can beef broth
1 cup water
1 package onion soup mix
1/2 cup quick-cooking barley (optional)
1 (14 ounce) can sliced mushrooms

Place stew meat (You can brown the stew meat first if you like or just place it in the crock pot without browning) and lima beans in crock pot. Mix all other ingredients together in a mixing bowl and pour into crock pot. Cook on low for 7 hours or high for 4 hours until meat is done. Makes 8 to 10 servings.

Three Bean Barbecue with Sausage

1 (15 ounce) can pork-n-beans, drained
1 (16 ounce) can chili beans, drained
1 (15 ounce) can pinto beans, drained
1 pound package smoked sausage or sausage or your choice, cut into chunks
1 onion, chopped
1/4 cup brown sugar
2 tablespoons Dijon mustard
2 tablespoons tomato ketchup
2 tablespoon molasses (I use sorghum. You could use any kind you like or even pancake syrup)
1 tablespoon Worcestershire sauce
few drops hot sauce

Drain beans and add to crockpot. Add remaining ingredients and mix well. Cook on low for 4 hours or high for 2 hours. Makes about 6 to 8 servings.

Other Main Dishes

Apricot Honey Pork Loin

1 (2 to 3 pound) pork loin
3 tablespoons cooking oil (I use Canola)
1/3 cup apricot preserves
1/4 cup honey
1/2 cup chopped onion (can use regular or green onions)
1 teaspoon salt
1/2 cup orange juice
1 tablespoon spicy brown mustard or mustard of your choice
1 teaspoon minced garlic
1/2 teaspoon black pepper
1 teaspoon soy sauce
fresh chopped parsley for garnish (optional)

Slice pork loin crosswise in 1/4 to 1/2 inch slices. Brown slices on both sides in oil on top of the stove. Whisk together remaining ingredients in a bowl. Place browned pork loin slices in a casserole dish and pour apricot and honey mixture over the slices. Cover with foil and bake in preheated 375 degree oven for 35 to 40 minutes. Can add chopped fresh parsley before serving. Makes approximately 8 servings depending on the size of your pork loin. Great served over rice or can serve with mashed potatoes.

Baked Chicken with Peaches

1 package chicken parts of your choice. (I use chicken thighs to make this but could use whatever parts you like)
3 tablespoons all-purpose flour
1/2 teaspoon salt
1/4 teaspoon black pepper
1/2 teaspoon ground cinnamon
1/2 teaspoon ground nutmeg
2 tablespoons butter or margarine
1 (1 pound) can sliced or halved peaches in juice

In a bowl whisk together the flour, salt, pepper, cinnamon and nutmeg. Spray a casserole dish with cooking spray. Place chicken parts in the casserole dish and sprinkle flour mixture over the parts. Cut the butter into pats and put it on top of each chicken piece. Bake uncovered in a preheated 375 degree oven for 35 to 40 minutes. Remove from oven and place peaches in casserole with chicken. Pour the peach juice over the chicken and peaches and put back in oven for 20 more minutes. Remove and spoon juice over chicken and serve.

Note: You could do this in a crock pot and add the peaches the last hour of cooking. Cook on low for about 7 hours or high for 4.

Baked Chicken with Sweet Potatoes

4 medium sized chicken breasts (could use other chicken parts in this recipe such as thighs or legs)
3 to 4 medium sweet potatoes, peeled and cut in chunks
1 medium onion, chopped (I use purple onion)
1 cup chicken broth
1/4 cup orange juice
1/4 cup honey
1 tablespoon olive oil
2 tablespoons spicy brown mustard
1 teaspoon thyme
1 teaspoon salt
1/2 teaspoon black pepper

Place the sweet potatoes and onion in a 2 to 3 quart baking dish with the chicken breasts on top. Whisk together the chicken broth, orange juice, honey, olive oil and mustard and thyme. Pour over the chicken and sweet potatoes. Sprinkle on the salt and pepper. Bake in preheated 400 degree oven covered for 35 minutes, remove cover, baste with gravy mixture and continue baking uncovered another 35 minutes or until sweet potatoes are tender and chicken is cooked. Makes 4 large servings. (If your chicken breasts are very large they could be halved to make 8 servings.)

Note: I take the broth from the chicken, strain, add 1 teaspoon cornstarch and bring to a boil on top of the stove stirring to keep from burning. This will thicken in about a minute. Pour into a gravy boat or small pitcher to serve over chicken.

Baked Spaghetti

1 1/2 pounds ground beef
1 green pepper, chopped
1 onion, chopped
1 teaspoon dried oregano or Italian seasoning
1/2 teaspoon black pepper
1 teaspoon salt
1 teaspoon minced garlic
1 (24 ounce) container Italian Spaghetti Sauce or pasta sauce of your choice
1 (8 ounce) package spaghetti
2 tablespoons butter
1 cup shredded Parmesan cheese, divided
1 (24 ounce) container cottage cheese
2 cups shredded mozzarella cheese

Brown ground beef, green pepper, and onion in a large skillet on top of the stove, drain. Add the oregano, black pepper, salt, minced garlic and Italian Spaghetti sauce to hamburger and stir to mix. Cook the spaghetti according to package directions, drain. Spray a 9 x 13 baking dish with cooking spray. Add the hot spaghetti and toss with the 2 tablespoons of butter and 1/2 cup Parmesan cheese. Spread spaghetti in bottom of dish and cover with entire container of cottage cheese. Spread the hamburger mixture over the cottage cheese. Top with the other 1/2 cup Parmesan cheese and the 2 cups of mozzarella cheese. Bake in preheated 400 degree oven covered for 30 minutes. Remove covering and cook for 15 more minutes. This makes about 10 to 12 servings and keeps great in the refrigerator for several days.

Barbecued Pork Chops

4 to 6 medium pork chops
1/2 cup brown sugar
1/4 cup honey
1/4 teaspoon garlic powder
1/4 teaspoon black pepper
2 tablespoons Dijon mustard

Mix all ingredients together except chops in a small bowl. Beat with a wire whisk until mixed well. Baste chops with sauce and grill basting several times while cooking.

Brown Sugar Meatloaf

Meatloaf Ingredients:
1 1/2 to 2 pounds ground beef
1 cup quick-cooking oats, uncooked
1/2 cup chopped green onions
1/3 cup chopped green pepper
1/2 cup chopped celery
1 tablespoon Worcestershire sauce
1/2 teaspoon liquid smoke
(optional)
Several drops hot sauce
2 teaspoons minced garlic
1 teaspoon salt
1/2 teaspoon black pepper
1 tablespoon Dijon mustard
1 (8 ounce) can tomato sauce,
divided (save the other half for the
sauce)
1 egg
1 tablespoon brown sugar.

Sauce Ingredients:
1/2 cup tomato sauce(the other half
of the 8 ounce can)
1/4 cup brown sugar
1/4 cup honey
2 tablespoons Dijon mustard

Mix all the meatloaf ingredients together in a large bowl. Shape into a loaf, place in casserole dish and bake uncovered in preheated 350 degree oven for 30 minutes.

Whisk sauce ingredients together in a bowl. Remove meatloaf after 30 minutes and pour sauce over the top. Raise oven temperature to 375 degrees and return meatloaf to oven. Cook 35 more minutes.

Serve any leftover sauce in pan over individual meatloaf slices.

Makes 6 to 8 servings.

Cheesy Hamburger Pie

1 lb. hamburger
1 small onion, chopped
1 small green pepper, chopped
1/2 teaspoon salt
Dash pepper
1/2 teaspoon minced garlic
1 teaspoon oregano
4 or 5 drops hot pepper sauce
1 1/2 to 2 cups of shredded cheese of your choice
1/2 cup Bisquick
1 cup milk
2 eggs

Preheat oven to 400 degrees. In a skillet, brown the hamburger, onion, and green pepper with the salt, pepper, garlic, oregano and hot sauce. Drain the hamburger mixture. Spray a 10 inch pie pan and spread the hamburger mixture in the bottom of the pan. Sprinkle 1 cup of the shredded cheese over the hamburger. In a small bowl, mix the Bisquick, milk, and eggs. Whisk together until smooth. Pour over the hamburger and cheese. Sprinkle the last 1/2 cup of shredded cheese over your mixture. Bake for 25 minutes. Makes 6 to 8 servings.

Chicken Nuggets with Homemade Ranch Dressing

Chicken Nugget Ingredients:
1 pound boneless, skinless chicken cut into bite sized pieces (can use chicken breasts, chicken fingers or whatever pieces you like)
1 cup all-purpose flour
1/2 teaspoon paprika
1/2 teaspoon ground mustard
1/2 cup plain bread crumbs
1/4 teaspoon black pepper
1/2 teaspoon salt
1/2 teaspoon garlic powder
Pinch cayenne (optional)
1/4 cup cooking oil
2 eggs

Ranch Dressing Ingredients:
1/2 cup buttermilk
1/2 cup sour cream
1/4 cup mayonnaise (could use Miracle Whip)
1 teaspoon dried parsley (could use fresh parsley)
1/2 teaspoon dried dill weed
1/2 teaspoon garlic powder
1/4 teaspoon black pepper
1/2 teaspoon salt
1/2 teaspoon dried chives (could use fresh chives)

Cut chicken into bite sized pieces and set aside. Whisk together the flour, paprika, mustard, bread crumbs, black pepper, salt garlic powder and cayenne in a bowl. In another bowl, beat the eggs until smooth. Heat cooking oil in skillet. Dip chicken pieces in flour mixture, then in beaten eggs and in flour mixture again. Make sure they are well coated. Cook six to seven minutes turning if needed. Remove with slotted spoon and drain on paper towels. Makes about 4 servings.

For Ranch Dressing whisk together all dressing ingredients and refrigerate for 2 to 3 hours. Makes about 1 1/4 cups dressing. Will keep in the refrigerator for several days.

Chicken Tenders with Honey Mustard Sauce

Chicken Tender Ingredients:
1 to 2 pounds boneless, skinless breast strips
1 cup all-purpose flour
3/4 cups oil
1 egg
3/4 cups milk
1 teaspoon thyme
1 teaspoon paprika
1 teaspoon cumin
1 teaspoon salt
1 teaspoon black pepper
1 teaspoon garlic powder
Pinch of cayenne (optional)

Honey Mustard Sauce:
1/4 cup Dijon mustard
1/4 cup honey
3/4 cup mayonnaise

Whisk together milk and egg in a bowl. In another bowl or pan whisk together to the flour and spices. Place tenders in the milk mixture. Heat oil in large skillet. Remove tenders from milk and dip in flour mixture. Cook in hot oil until crusty and tender. About 10 to 15 minutes on each side. Makes about 6 servings.

For Honey Mustard Sauce whisk ingredients together in a bowl, will keep in refrigerator for several days. Makes 1 1/4 cups.

Cube Steak and Onion Gravy

1 1/2 to 2 pounds cube steak
1/4 cup flour
1/4 teaspoon black pepper
1/4 teaspoon salt
1/4 teaspoon garlic powder
1/2 cup oil
1 (14 ounce) can beef broth
1 onion, cut into rings
1 package dry onion soup mix

Mix flour, pepper, salt, and garlic powder in a shallow dish. Coat cube steak with flour mixture. In a skillet heat oil and cook steak about five minutes on each side until brown and done on inside. Remove steak from pan. Add beef broth, onion, and dry onion soup mix to pan and cook until onions are done. Can thicken gravy with a little of the leftover flour if you want it thicker. Serve gravy as a side or pour over steak. Makes 4 to 6 servings.

Note: This gravy is great over mashed potatoes or biscuits, too.

Fried Catfish Fillets

1 to 2 pounds fresh catfish fillets
Milk or buttermilk for soaking
3 eggs
1 cup all-purpose flour or can use cornmeal
1 teaspoon salt
1/2 teaspoon black pepper
1/4 teaspoon garlic powder
3/4 cup oil

Place fillets in a 9 x 13 pan and cover with milk or buttermilk. Let soak for about an hour in the refrigerator. In a large bowl mix flour, salt, pepper, and garlic powder. In a smaller bowl whisk eggs until smooth. Remove fish from milk and discard the milk. Dip fillets in egg and then in flour mixture. Make sure you have about 1/2 inch of oil in your skillet. Fry on each side until golden brown; about 6 or 7 minutes. Drain and serve. Makes 4 to 6 servings.

Fried Chicken Livers

1 pound chicken livers
1 cup buttermilk (could use regular milk)
1 cup self-rising flour (could use all-purpose)
1 teaspoon garlic powder
1 teaspoon black pepper
1 teaspoon salt
pinch cayenne or a few drops hot sauce (optional)
1/8 teaspoon cumin (optional)
cooking oil (I use Canola and about 1/2 cup)

Put the chicken livers in the buttermilk and let soak for about 3 or 4 minutes. Mix flour, garlic powder, salt, pepper, cayenne and cumin in a shallow bowl. Dredge chicken liver in flour until totally covered. Heat oil in skillet. Fry livers turning often until crispy. Remove from skillet and drain. Makes 4 servings.

Gravy from Drippings: If you have any flour left over from dredging the livers put it in the drippings left in the frying pan. You need about 1/4 cup flour. I leave the crumbs in the skillet with the drippings, add the flour and stir to soak up the oil. Add about 1 1/2 cups milk and a teaspoon black pepper. Bring to a boil, stirring to keep from burning and cook until gravy thickens to desired consistency. Serve over chicken livers. Makes about 1 1/2 cups of gravy.

Fried Pork Chops and Gravy

5 or 6 center cut pork chops (about 3 lbs.)
1 cup flour
1/2 teaspoon black pepper
1/2 teaspoon salt
1/2 teaspoon garlic powder
3 to 4 tablespoons oil for frying or bacon drippings
2 1/2 cups water
1/2 cup milk

Put your cup of flour in a shallow pan and whisk in black pepper, salt and garlic powder. Dredge the pork chops in the flour until fully covered on both sides. Heat oil in a large skillet. Brown chops on both sides, turn down heat, cover your skillet and let cook for about 15 minutes until chops are thoroughly cooked. Remove chops from pan, place on plate and cover to keep warm. Make sure you have at least 1/4 cup of drippings in the pan (can add more oil, if needed) Add enough flour to make a roux or paste (I use any leftover flour from dredging plus more if needed). Cook and stir until flour is browned. Add water and milk. Bring to boil and cook to desired thickness for gravy. Makes about 2 1/2 cups gravy. Serve over chops, potatoes, rice, etc. Makes 4 to 6 servings.

Note: You can return chops to the gravy and simmer for 10 to 15 minutes covered if you want to serve it this way. I like doing the gravy separate as some people don't like gravy on their pork chops.

Impossible Chili Pie

1 pound lean ground beef
1/2 cup chopped onion
1/2 cup chopped green pepper (optional)
1 (15.5 ounce) can chili beans, drained
1 cup frozen corn
1 (4 ounce) can green chilies, drained
1/4 teaspoon black pepper
1/4 teaspoon salt
1 teaspoon minced garlic
1 teaspoon chili powder
Pinch cayenne or few drops hot sauce
1/2 cup chunky salsa
1 cup shredded cheese of your choice, divided
3/4 cup Bisquick
3 eggs
1 cup milk
Green pepper rings for garnish (optional)

Brown ground beef, onion and green pepper in a skillet on top of the stove. Drain and return to pan. Add drained chili beans, corn, green chilies, pepper, salt, garlic, chili powder, hot sauce and salsa. Mix all ingredients together and heat for about 5 minutes. Spray a 10 inch pie plate or can use a 9 x 9 square baking dish. Pour ingredients into dish and sprinkle 1/2 cup of the shredded cheese on top. Whisk together the Bisquick, eggs and milk. Pour over the cheese. Add the remaining cheese and green pepper rings. Bake in preheated 400 degree oven for 25 to 30 minutes. Makes about 8 servings.

Lima Beans with Ham over Rice

1 (1 pound) bag of large dried lima beans
1 large ham hock with some meat still on the bone or 1 cup chopped ham
1 medium onion, chopped
1/2 teaspoon minced garlic
1/2 teaspoon black pepper
1 teaspoon salt
2 – 4 cups rice, cooked according to package directions depending on how many people you are serving

Rinse and sort beans, soak overnight in a large pot of water. Next morning, drain soak water and rinse beans. Add six cups of fresh water, the chopped onion, garlic, pepper, and ham or ham hock. Simmer beans with lid tilted on pot for about 3 hours until tender, then add salt. (I always salt dried beans after they are done. They take longer to cook if you salt them during the cooking process.) If using a ham hock, remove it from pot and take the ham from the bone and add back to the beans. Serve over rice. Makes 8 to 10 servings.

Pan Fried Cod Fish Fillets

1 pound cod fish fillets
3/4 cup buttermilk (could use regular milk)
1 cup cornmeal
1 teaspoon salt
1/2 teaspoon black pepper
1/2 teaspoon garlic powder (optional)
1/4 cup oil (I use Canola)

Mix the cornmeal, salt, pepper and garlic powder together in a shallow pan. Dip fillets in buttermilk, then in cornmeal mixture. Brown on both sides in hot oil. Turn heat down to medium and let cook about 5 to 10 minutes. Makes 4 to 6 servings.

Red Beans, Smoked Sausage and Rice

1 (1 pound) bag dried small red beans
8 cups water
4 chicken bouillon cubes (can use 2 less cups of water and add one can of chicken broth)
1 teaspoon bacon drippings (optional)
1 ham hock
1 teaspoon minced garlic
1 small onion, chopped
1 teaspoon thyme
1 teaspoon black pepper
1/2 teaspoon ground sage
1 pound smoked sausage, cut into rounds or pieces
1 bay leaf
1 teaspoon salt
Long grain rice or rice of your choice

Rinse the beans and put in dutch oven or large pot. (I do not soak these beans) Add water and remaining ingredients except for salt. Bring to a boil. Reduce heat, cover and simmer on low for about 2 hours. Add salt before serving.   Serve over rice. Makes 8 to 10 servings.

Salmon Patties

1 (15 ounce) can salmon, undrained
1 egg
1 sleeve of saltine crackers, crushed
3/4 cup cooking oil (I use canola oil) for cooking

Heat the oil in a large skillet. Combine the rest of the ingredients in a large mixing bowl. Using your hands mix the ingredients together and shape into patties. Place the patties in the hot oil and brown on each side. Turn the heat down and continue cooking on low for about 20 minutes turning often. Let cook until the patties are brown and crusty. Makes 4 to 6 servings.

Smoked Sausage and Roasted Vegetables

4 or 5 potatoes, peeled and cut into chunks
1 large green pepper, seeded and cut into rings
1 large onion, peeled and cut into rings
3 or 4 carrots, cut into pieces
1 (1 pound) package Smoked Sausage, cut into pieces
3 tablespoons oil
1 teaspoon salt
1/2 teaspoon black pepper
1/2 teaspoon garlic powder
1/2 teaspoon dried basil

Use a 9 x 13 baking dish lined with foil and sprayed with cooking spray. Toss vegetables with oil, sprinkle on salt, pepper, garlic powder and basil. Cook in preheated 450 degree oven for 30 minutes. Remove from oven add sausage. Cook for 15 more minutes. Makes about 6 servings.

Note: You can do this with all kinds of vegetables. Use whatever you have on hand.

Spaghetti with Meat Sauce

1 1/2 pounds ground beef
1 onion, chopped
1 green pepper, chopped
1 (10 ounce) can diced tomatoes with green chilis
2 (8 ounce) cans tomato sauce
1 (13.25 ounce) can mushroom stems and pieces, drained
1 teaspoon minced garlic
3 teaspoons dried oregano
1 teaspoon sugar
Salt to taste
Parmesan cheese (optional)

Brown ground beef, onion, and green pepper. Drain. Add remaining ingredients except Parmesan cheese and simmer about 45 minutes. Serve over spaghetti cooked according to package directions. Makes enough sauce for approximately 6 servings. Can top with Parmesan cheese.

Note: This could be made in the crock pot as well. Just brown your meat with your onions and peppers, then add to slow cooker.

Spicy Indian Baked Chicken

4 boneless, skinless chicken breasts (could use other chicken parts)
1/4 cup yellow cornmeal
1/4 teaspoon salt
1/4 teaspoon paprika
1/4 teaspoon ground cloves
1/4 teaspoon turmeric
1/4 teaspoon cumin
1/4 teaspoon coriander
Pinch cayenne pepper (can add more)
1/2 cup dry roasted peanuts, finely ground
1/4 cup coconut, finely ground
1/2 cup buttermilk
4 tablespoons butter or margarine, melted

Combine yellow cornmeal with salt, paprika, cloves, turmeric, cumin, coriander, and cayenne in a shallow pan. Mix well with wire whisk. Grind peanuts and coconut finely. I used my coffee grinder. You could use a blender or a food processor, too. Add peanuts and coconut to cornmeal mixture and mix together with a spoon or whisk. Pour 1/2 cup buttermilk in a separate bowl. Dip chicken in milk and then in peanut mixture. Spray a baking dish and add chicken to the dish. Drizzle melted butter over the chicken. Bake in preheated 375 degree oven 55-60 minutes or until chicken is done in center. Makes 4 servings.

Stuffed Green Peppers

6 large green peppers or 8 medium, tops removed, seeded (save the tops to add to stuffing)
1 pound lean ground beef
1 medium onion, chopped
1 teaspoon oregano or Italian seasoning
1 teaspoon Worcestershire sauce
1/2 teaspoon black pepper
1/2 teaspoon salt
1/2 teaspoon minced garlic
1/2 teaspoon dried basil
1 (4 ounce) can green chilies, drained
1 (14.5 ounce) can diced tomatoes, drain and save the juice
1/2 cup minute rice (can use regular rice but need to cook it first if you do)
1 (4 ounce) can tomato sauce (optional)
Cheese for tops of peppers, about 1/2 cup shredded (your choice of type of cheese)

In a large pot of boiling water, after you have removed the seeds and stems, boil the peppers for five minutes to soften them up. Remove from water and drain on paper towels. Brown the hamburger, onion, chopped pepper tops and drain if needed. Add the oregano, Worcestershire sauce, pepper, salt, garlic, basil, green chilies, drained diced tomatoes and minute rice. Simmer until rice is tender or about 5 minutes. Fill your peppers with the hamburger mixture. (If you are using the tomato sauce pour it over the filled peppers. Some people like a lot of tomato taste and use the sauce) Pour the drained tomato juice that you saved from the diced tomatoes into the bottom of your casserole dish. Bake peppers in preheated 400 degree oven for 20 minutes. Remove and add shredded cheese to top of each pepper. Return to oven for five more minutes until cheese melts. This recipe makes 6 to 8 stuffed peppers. I would cut in half if only making four.

Note: You could use ground turkey in this recipe.

Sweet and Sour Hamburger Steak and Gravy

1 pound ground beef
1 egg
1/2 teaspoon salt
1/4 teaspoon black pepper
1/2 teaspoon garlic powder
1 teaspoon minced onion
1/2 cup quick oats
1/2 teaspoon Italian seasoning or oregano
2 tablespoons oil
2 tablespoons brown sugar
2 tablespoons flour
1/4 cup finely chopped onion
1 (8 ounce) can tomato sauce
1 (4 ounce) can mushroom stems and pieces, drained
1/4 cup chopped green pepper
1 teaspoon Worcestershire sauce
1 tablespoon Dijon mustard
1/2 cup water

In a mixing bowl combine the ground beef, egg, salt, pepper, garlic powder, minced onion, oats and Italian seasoning. Make into patties. (I usually make 4 patties out of a pound of hamburger). Brown the hamburger patties in the oil in a skillet. Drain. Mix together the brown sugar, flour, onion, tomato sauce, mushrooms, green pepper, Worcestershire sauce, Dijon mustard, and water. Pour over the hamburger steaks in the skillet and simmer for about 20 to 25 minutes. If you need more liquid, add a little more water. Makes 4 servings. Serve the gravy over mashed potatoes, rice or pasta.

Baked Chicken Thighs with Rice

6 to 8 boneless, skinless chicken thighs (you could make this with any parts of the chicken or even a whole chicken)
2 teaspoons minced garlic
1/2 cup butter or margarine
3 tablespoons soy sauce
1/4 teaspoon salt
1/4 teaspoon black pepper
1 tablespoon dried parsley flakes

Spray a casserole dish. Mix all ingredients except chicken together in a microwave bowl and microwave on high for about one minute or until butter melts. Mix well and pour over chicken. Bake at 375 degrees for 50 minutes, turning chicken half way through baking. Serve over rice.

Beef Liver Smothered with Onions

1 pound beef liver
3 – 4 tablespoons bacon grease (can use butter or margarine if you don't have the grease)
1/2 teaspoon salt
1/4 teaspoon black pepper
1/4 teaspoon garlic powder
1 – 2 large onions, peeled and cut into rings
1/2 cup flour
1 cup water

Put the flour into a shallow dish and add salt, pepper, and garlic powder. Mix well. Add grease to skillet and have hot. Dredge liver in flour and fry on both sides until brown. Sprinkle onion rings on top of the liver in the pan and add about a cup of water. Cover and simmer until beef it tender about 7 or 8 minutes. Makes about 6 servings.

Dijion Onion Chicken and Gravy

1 (6 ounce) can Crispy Fried Onions
2 tablespoons Dijon Mustard
4 tablespoons all-purpose flour
1 egg
4 or 5 chicken thighs

Spray a 9 x 13 baking dish. Pour onions into a large plastic bag and add the flour to the onion. Mash the bag until onions are mostly crumbs and well mixed with the flour. In a bowl whisk the mustard and egg together. Dip chicken pieces into egg mixture and then into crumbs. Place in baking dish and bake in preheated 400 degree oven for 30 – 45 minutes until chicken is done and crispy. Makes 4 servings.

For Gravy: Pour drippings from baking dish into a frying pan. Add about 3 tablespoons of flour and mix well with burner on high. Add 1 1/2 cups milk, salt and pepper to taste and bring to a rapid boil. Cook until thickens. Pour over chicken pieces and serve.

Grilled Tilapia Fillets

4 frozen tilapia fillets, thawed (could use fresh)
1/2 cup chopped onion
1/2 cup chopped red pepper (could use green pepper)
2 bay leaves
1/2 teaspoon garlic salt
2 tablespoon butter or margarine
1/2 cup tomato ketchup
Salt and Pepper

Cook pepper and onion in butter in skillet on top of the stove until tender. (Don't overcook). Add ketchup, garlic salt and bay leaves. Simmer for 10 to 15 minutes. Place tilapia fillets in Reynolds wrap, sprinkle with salt and pepper. Pour the peppers and onions over the fillets, seal edges of foil. Place on hot grill, turning foil package once during cooking. Grill about six minutes on each side. Makes 4 servings.

Honey Baked Chicken Breast

2 to 4 boneless chicken breasts (could use thighs or legs, too)
2 cups corn flakes, crushed
1/3 cup honey
Salt and pepper

Put corn flakes in a plastic bag and crush as fine as you can get them. Add salt and black pepper to crumbs and pour into a bowl.   Put honey in a second bowl. Dip chicken in honey making sure it is fully coated, then in corn flake crumbs.

Spray baking dish and bake chicken in preheated 375 degree oven for about 60 minutes until golden brown. Makes 2 to 4 servings.

Oven Baked Pork Chops

2 to 4 boneless pork chops
1 tablespoon brown sugar
1 teaspoon Dijon mustard
1 teaspoon Worcestershire sauce
1 tablespoon molasses
1 teaspoon minced garlic
1 egg
1/4 teaspoon salt
1/4 teaspoon black pepper
Bread crumbs of your choice or all-purpose flour

Whisk all ingredients together except bread crumbs until you have a smooth sauce. Dip each chop in liquid and then in bread crumbs. Bake in preheated 375 degree oven for 45 minutes or until chops are done in the middle. Makes 2 to 4 servings.

Index

CASSEROLES _____ 7

American Shepherds Pie, 12
Baked Chicken with Peaches, 13
Baked Sweet Potato Casserole, 14
Baked Sweet Potatoes, 15
Barley Casserole, 16
Black-Eyed Peas and Smoked Sausage, 46
Broccoli Casserole, 17
Cabbage Roll Casserole, 18
Cabbage, Ham and Spaghetti Casserole, 19
Cheesy Bacon Yellow Squash Casserole, 20
Cheesy Hash Brown Casserole, 9
Cheesy Macaroni and Cheese, 46
Cheesy Tater Tot Casserole, 21
Cheesy Tuna Casserole, 22
Chicken Salad Casserole, 47
Chicken Tortilla Chip Casserole, 23
Creamy Cauliflower Casserole, 24
Easy Cheesy Breakfast Casserole, 25
Garlic Cheese Grits, 26
Ham, Potato and Broccoli Casserole, 27
Ham, Spinach and Pasta Casserole, 28
Hamburger 'N Shells Italia, 29
Hamburger Supreme Casserole, 30
Hash Brown and Sausage Breakfast Casserole, 31
Hawaiian Beans and Wieners, 32
Hearty Chicken Pot Pie, 33
Hearty Mexican Casserole, 34
Italian Eggplant Casserole, 35
Mashed Potato Casserole, 36
Orange Beet Casserole, 47
Pineapple Casserole, 11
Ritzy Brussels Sprouts, 37
Salmon Pasta Casserole, 38
Sausage, Tomato and Cheese Grits Casserole, 39
Savory Corn Pudding, 48
Scalloped Corn Casserole, 40
Scalloped Potatoes with Cheese, 41

Spicy Apricot Chicken, 48
Sweet Potato Pone, 49
Swiss Chicken Casserole, 42
Yummy Corn Casserole, 43
Zucchini Pasta Casserole, 45
Zucchini and Tomato Casserole, 44

OTHER MAIN DISHES _____ 135
Apricot Honey Pork Loin, 136
Baked Chicken Thighs with Rice, 159
Baked Chicken with Peaches, 137
Baked Chicken with Sweet Potatoes, 138
Baked Spaghetti, 139
Barbecued Pork Chops, 140
Beef Liver Smothered with Onions, 159
Brown Sugar Meatloaf, 141
Cheesy Hamburger Pie, 142
Chicken Nuggets with Homemade Ranch Dressing, 143
Chicken Tenders with Honey Mustard Sauce, 144
Cube Steak and Onion Gravy, 145
Dijion Onion Chicken and Gravy, 160
Fried Catfish Fillets, 146
Fried Chicken Livers, 147
Fried Pork Chops and Gravy, 148
Grilled Tilapia Fillets, 160
Honey Baked Chicken Breast, 161
Impossible Chili Pie, 149
Lima Beans with Ham over Rice, 150
Oven Baked Pork Chops, 161
Pan Fried Cod Fish Fillets, 151
Red Beans, Smoked Sausage and Rice, 152
Salmon Patties, 153
Smoked Sausage and Roasted Vegetables, 154
Spaghetti with Meat Sauce, 155
Spicy Indian Baked Chicken, 156
Stuffed Green Peppers, 157
Sweet and Sour Hamburger Steak and Gravy, 158

SIDE DISHES _____ 51
Baked Parmesan Zucchini Fries, 62
Brown Sugar Glazed Baby Carrots, 62
Cornbread Dressing and Giblet Gravy, 56

Creamed Cucumbers, 63
Creamy Mashed Potatoes, 63
Cucumbers in Vinegar, 64
Favorite Coleslaw, 64
Fresh Mustard and Turnip Greens, 65
Fried Green Tomatoes and Fried Okra, 53
Great Deviled Eggs, 57
Green Beans and Potatoes, 58
Macaroni and Tomatoes, 59
Maple Baked Beans with Sausage, 60
Old Fashioned Ice Box Coleslaw, 65
Parmesan Baked Potato Wedges, 61
Roasted Brussels Sprouts with Bacon and Walnuts, 55
Roasted Potato Bites, 66
Southern Baked Beans, 66

SKILLET MEALS _____ 67
Beans and Franks with a Twist, 74
Beef Stoganoff, 92
Cabbage, Bacon and Potato Skillet, 75
Cheesy Bacon and Cabbage Skillet, 76
Cheesy Pepperoni Pizza Pasta Skillet, 77
Cheesy Sausage Tortellini Skillet, 69
Cheesy Smoked Sausage Pasta Skillet, 78
Chicken Creole, 79
Fried Apples, 92
Fried Cabbage with Sausage, 80
Fried Corn, 81
Hamburger Creamed Gravy, 93
Hamburger Steak and Gravy, 82
Italian Sausage and Manwich Sandwich or Skillet Meal, 83
Okra and Potatoes Supreme, 71
Peach Mango Pork Chops and Rice, 84
Pork Chop and Apple Skillet, 85
Quick and Easy Hamburger Goulash, 86
Sausage and Rice Skillet Meal, 93
Sausage, Pasta and Cheese Skillet, 87
Smoked Sausage, Tomatoes and Okra Skillet, 88
Spanish Rice and Smoked Sausage, 89
Spicy Shrimp Creole, 73
Sweet and Sour Pork Skillet, 90
Zucchini Beef Skillet, 91

SLOW COOKER RECIPES — 95

Apricot Ribs, 127
Barbecued Chicken Breast, 98
Beef Stew, 99
Beef and Tomato Gravy, 127
Beer Brats and Sauerkraut, 100
Cabbage and Ham, 128
Cabbage, Potatoes and Smoke Sausage, 128
Cajun Beef Roast, 101
Chicken, Apple, Potatoes and Cabbage, 129
Chicken, Broccoli and Pasta, 102
Chicken, Potatoes and Broccoli, 103
Coca Cola Pork Chops, 104
Corned Beef and Cabbage, 105
Country Style Ribs, 106
Cranberry Chicken, 129
Cranberry Orange Pork Loin Roast, 97
Dijon Chicken Breast, 107
Fiesta Chicken, 108
Ham and Potatoes, 130
Hamburger and Beans Supreme, 109
Homemade Applesauce, 110
Honey Soy Pork Chops, 111
Italian Sausage Spaghetti, 112
Juicy Beef Roast, 113
Manwich Chicken, 130
Picante Chicken, 114
Polish Sausage, Sauerkraut and Potatoes, 115
Pork Roast and Sauerkraut, 131
Pork Roast and White Beans, 116
Pulled Pork Barbecue, 117
Pumpkin Chili, 118
Roast Beef and Vegetables, 131
Round Steak and Gravy, 119
Round Steak with Peppers and Onions, 132
Santa Fe Stew, 120
Sausage and Veggies with Peppers, 121
Sausage, White Bean and Pasta Soup, 122
Smoked Sausage Gumbo, 123
Spicy Apricot Chicken, 132
Spicy Pork Loin Roast, 124
Stew Meat and Lima Beans, 133

Sweet Potatoes, Pineapple and Cranberries, 125
Three Bean Barbecue with Sausage, 133
Zesty Chicken, 126

All Rights Reserved. No part of this Publication may be reproduced or distributed in any form or by any means, electronic or mechanical, or stored in a database or retrieval system without prior permission from Retro Rodeo Publishing, LLC.
All photography Copyright Judy Yeager.